This is the story of a remarkable man – successful businessman, skilled negotiator and loyal friend. He has also driven a golf ball further than anyone else on record, but, as his book clearly shows, he has reason to be proud of his achievements in a much wider field. Life, as Tommy Campbell insists, is 'not only about throwing cricket balls, hitting golf balls, or knocking people out...' His own life, described in his own inimitable and exhilarating style, provides eloquent testimony to that.

                The Rt. Hon. the Lord Chalfont OBE MC PC

STAYING THE COURSE

W.T. (Tommie) Campbell

MINERVA PRESS
ATLANTA LONDON SYDNEY

STAYING THE COURSE
Copyright © W.T. (Tommie) Campbell 1998

All Rights Reserved

No part of this book may be reproduced in any form,
by photocopying or by any electronic or mechanical means,
including information storage or retrieval systems,
without permission in writing from both the copyright owner
and the publisher of this book.

ISBN 0 75410 496 6

First Published 1998 by
MINERVA PRESS
Sixth Floor
Canberra House
315-317 Regent Street
London W1R 7YB

Printed in Great Britain for Minerva Press

STAYING THE COURSE

To Wendy,
who persuaded me to take up my pen.

About the Author

Sports followers, and particularly those associated with golf, will know of the skill and sportsmanship of Tommie Campbell.

Always active as a player, administrator and commentator at the highest level, he has played with distinction all over the world. A low handicap player for many years, he is still far from finished, having won two major match-play tournaments in 1995.

Norris McWhirter, publisher of the *Guinness Book of Records*, described Tommie as, 'pound for pound one of the greatest athletes of modern time' when he entered that book with a world long drive record of three hundred and ninety-two yards in 1964.[1]

It did not stop there, because Tommie went on to win further events in the USA and Europe, and then in August 1990 he drove the thirteenth hole at Royal Cinque Ports in Deal, a distance of four hundred and twenty yards.

Born in Dublin, Ireland, Tommie is married with three children, and for the last ten years he has lived in the UK. His explosive energy is not confined to sport – he has stamped his personality on those areas of business where his story is one of success. His beginnings were in the raw wool trade, where he reached a top six position worldwide. In addition, on three separate occasions he was voted by the

---

[1] *Guinness Book of World Records*, 1990 edition, London, Guinness Publishing Ltd, 1990. Copyright and trademark in records published in the *Guinness Book of World Records* belongs to Guinness Publishing Ltd.

Committee of Supervisors in the USA carpet market as being 'most reliable supplier'.

From there, always full of ideas, Tommie progressed into the total carpet trade, opening the first carpet 'cash and carry' in the sixties and building the most modern dyeing and spinning mill in the seventies. Today his unique blend of sports marketing and management, allied to his manufacturing technology, is transforming the synthetic turf systems of the sports and leisure industry. This is an area which Tommie has always held as containing the best opportunities and development potential for the future.

What has emerged is a person respected worldwide, whose experience as a negotiator has seen him lead a number of delegations all over the globe. Tommie the organiser is peerless and, as in his sporting achievements, always seems to have plenty of time and balance no matter how intense the pressure.

Today the enthusiasm still burns as bright as ever, be he on the golf course or in the boardroom. Sunningdale is now his home club although he is a member of other great courses, such as Royal Cinque Ports and Portmarnock. Twenty-six years in the *Guinness Book of Records*, a record in itself, has not changed him. He will always be regarded by those who know him as a tough competitor and a loyal friend.

At last Tommie has been persuaded to write a book, which is looked forward to with great interest as being the story of the full and fascinating life of one of sport and commerce's greatest characters.

Acknowledgements

The extract from the *Guinness Book of Records* on page 5 and reference to the copyrighted world record on pages 93–102 is reprinted with kind permission from the publishers, Guinness Publishing Limited.

News items are reproduced with kind permission from the *Irish Times*.

Contents

Introduction		xi
One	Negotiating the Foothills	15
Two	Starting the Ascent	28
Three	Swastikas in Dublin	40
Four	Work and Some Play	45
Five	Go It Alone	58
Six	The Gathering Storm	72
Seven	The Hereafter	80
Eight	The World Famous Golf Drive	93
Nine	South Africa	103
Ten	So What!	114
Eleven	Never Meet Your Heroes	120
Twelve	A Price to Pay	128
Thirteen	Keep On Keeping On	135

Introduction

Some long for it, others have it thrust upon them, more than a few would willingly sacrifice their lives for it, and there are those who would rather be known by their crimes than not known at all – they call it fame.

I suppose one way to become famous is to hold a place in the *Guinness Book of Records* for twenty-six years. It attracts cynicism, admiration, curiosity and contempt and really draws back the curtain to reveal all human emotions. Your life is no longer your own, you must learn to cope with all types of vicissitudes, and one thing you must never forget is that a catalogue of any weaknesses, infirmities or bad news will go with you to the grave.

Many of these I have experienced in some form or another, beginning before I was born when my father was nearly killed by a Black and Tan bullet at Croke Park, Dublin, during the 1920 All-Ireland Football Final. Why was he there – why were the Black and Tans there, and why did they shoot at him? There is a remarkable similarity between what was happening then and what is happening in Ireland today.

Those were terrible times, and nearly seven years later I entered them weighing over nine pounds and baptised into a religion which was not the right persuasion as far as the majority of people in Southern Ireland were concerned. Years of violence, beatings and humiliation followed, all because I came into the world as a Protestant. Probably unknowingly at the time I gathered a strength both mentally and physically from these incidents, which has stood me in good stead all of my life.

As well as having described me as 'pound for pound one of the greatest athletes of modern time', Norris McWhirter also said that I was born with an ability to store up a massive fund of energy from the tips of my toes to the tips of my fingers, and release it all in one great explosion of power. This of course was said after my record long drive in 1964, when I was only five feet eight inches tall and weighing ten and a half stone. But this book will show other remarkable incidents, including three which took place before I was twelve years old involving a cricket-ball throwing competition and two episodes in a boxing ring.

Life, however, is not only about throwing cricket balls, hitting golf balls, or knocking people out – unless you are being paid for it! In those days there were no big sport impresarios around, nor the incentive to become a professional.

If I have had some success in my life so far, then I have also had adversity, a lot of which was self-imposed. It is easy with hindsight to look back at these things, but at the time they were all very real. Thanks to De Valera's artful diplomatic management in the thirties my earlier years were difficult, not only for me but for my family. The self-imposed economic war with Britain brought untold hardships, and when my grandmother died intestate, having married for the second time to a ne'er-do-well naval captain, the family estates went to him. Needless to say we never saw a penny!

I remember my father saying that he could not afford a higher education for me, but that a job was available to me in a business owned by a relative. I did not take up this offer, much to the chagrin of my family, and especially the relation who owned it. I often wonder what would have happened if I had accepted.

Instead I was off on my own into the raw wool business,

and many things have happened since then which I believe would be an inspiration to all young people starting out today. Long hours brought their own rewards – the creation of one of the top six carpet wool firms in the world, starting the first carpet 'cash and carry' which brought into existence the impulse buy – now accepted worldwide, travelling millions of miles, meeting people like Molotov, and of course getting married and entering the *Guinness Book of Records*.

One of the conditions of fortune is misfortune, and my misfortunes have included bad judgement of partners at the start, due to lack of experience, being involved in three air crashes, having my business burned down by persons unknown – probably terrorists, being set up by a government on a phoney charge which grew into one of the most famous court cases in Irish legal history, and getting over a nervous breakdown on my feet.

From the beginning of my business career I made a number of resolutions. Two of these were that I would always travel first class on the basis that if I could not afford it I was a failure, and that I would retire at the age of forty-five. Both of these came to pass, except in the latter case not completely, because I became involved in sport and leisure – an area not unfamiliar to me. I was one of the co-founders of the Freedom in Sport movement, which took me to many parts of the world, including some forty-odd trips to South Africa. When I took eighty-six media people from sixteen different countries in 1983, South Africa's 'Mr Rugby', Dr Danie Craven, said, 'Future generations will thank Tommie Campbell – we have much to thank him for.' Another experience in South Africa was my confrontation with Bishop Tutu over his policy of stopping young children from going to school. I remember my simple question to him in Johannesburg was, 'What will you do with ten million illiterate teenagers in a few years time?' A question which did not please him.

Six months earlier, on a trip to Australia and New Zealand, I had a famous interview with Alex Veysey of the *New Zealand Times*. Among the many things which he wrote about me was one sentence which had significance thereafter – 'I have heard the voice of sportsmen demanding fairness to play and be suitably rewarded, but the missionary fervour of Tommie Campbell sends out an international message which sports administrators will ignore at their cost.'

Life has had many funny moments, with characters like Brendan Behan, Sean O'Sullivan and a host of others who were around at the time. Being in the *Guinness Book of Records* also brought many incidents upon which to reflect, like eleven proposals of marriage by post, hundreds of letters – mostly challenges, others of disbelief – and many invitations from all sorts of people, including kings. Everybody wants to know you!

In the midst of all this one thing will always stand out in my mind. When I was in Durban in 1968 a young black boy came up to me with a rusty bucket and asked if I would fill it with sea water for him. Being my first time in South Africa I asked him why he could not do it himself – never realising he was not allowed on the beach.

The title of this book has been precisely chosen – it is not just an autobiography. I believe it is the story of a person whose boundless energies, allied to a survivor instinct, afforded him one of the fullest and most controversial lives within the worlds of business and sport. It has allowed him to witness and examine many of the problems which have beset industry and politics in different parts of the world.

How I wish that I were thirty years younger now, but with the same knowledge!

Chapter One

Negotiating the Foothills

A wallop on the chin in a boxing ring is not unusual, but when it comes from a lady's handbag as you are sitting on a stool in one of the corners it soon makes you begin to wonder what is going on.

She had it in for me because I had just knocked out her son in the first round of the school boxing championships. When it happened she came charging down the aisle shouting, 'Get that animal out of the ring!' Within seconds she was pounding up the steps into the ring, brushing aside with ease the two flabbergasted officials who tried to stop her, then as she reached my corner, bang!

'It must have been an accident, a little fellow like Tommie weighing only seventy-three pounds could not knock anyone out,' I heard the master saying to the good lady. 'Your son is okay, don't worry,' and indeed he was, and continued to be one of my friends for many years.

This was just one odd happening of many in my life. Johnny Nelson, the school coach and a former middleweight champion, told me years later he realised then I was something different, and potentially dangerous in any ring. The morning after the boxing match the headmaster had the same opinion, when he told me as I stood before his desk that I was banned from boxing but could continue to use the gym for training.

'That's that,' said Johnny Nelson, neither of us realising

for a moment a much more dramatic incident was to take place in that same ring a few years later.

I was very happy in that school, and often feel what happened on my very first day helped towards that. New boys had to go through the rigors of an initiation which I became aware of during the first break, a ceremony which involved being ducked head first into a toilet. Two rather large louts grabbed my jacket and proceeded to frogmarch me across the yard to the appointed place in one of the school washrooms. In attendance was a collection of other minnows, which didn't bother me particularly as my mind was concentrating on how I would handle the situation.

Where the ability came from I don't know, but I have always managed to remain cool and calm under pressure, and at that moment my brain, I remember, was as sharp as a razor. I decided to attack.

First came the warning – these were my exact words, 'I will not allow you to do this to me. If you don't let go – now – I am going to kill you.' Loud guffaws of laughter followed which quickly changed to screams as I lashed out and taught them a lesson they would not forget. In fact I found out one of them had a fractured jaw – unfortunately the news came from the headmaster, next day, in his study. However, he pronounced it as having been undue provocation, and added he would expel any boys found participating in this type of carry-on in the future.

Two things I have never tolerated – bullying and cruelty to animals, both of which aversions I inherited from my mother and father. One occasion which comes to my mind occurred while fishing with my dad near Dublin. We were getting ready to start out to sea when we noticed some boys had captured a bird, which they were holding in their boat at the bottom of the steps about twenty feet below us. Straight away my father ordered them to let the bird go, but the response was the usual verbiage one would expect.

Then I noticed that he had picked up an old anchor and was holding it suspended above them. 'If you don't let go, I'm going to drop this straight into you.' They didn't believe him, but they didn't know my dad, who let go of the anchor which went right through the bottom of the boat. It quickly sank, but the bird got away.

Life for me up to this time had been very hard because of the terrible persecution and violence I had to endure living in Ireland. Luck played a part in my being there at all because had the bullet fired at my father in Croke Park Stadium on Sunday 21st November, 1920 been a fraction to the left, he would have been killed and I would never have been born. What was all this about? Why did it happen, and what was my dad doing there anyway?

What was it all about? The troubles between England and Ireland were in full flight. On the Irish side were the old IRA led by Michael Collins, and on the other the 'Black and Tans,' so called because of the odd uniforms they wore. They were mostly highly paid ex-servicemen sent over by Lloyd George, then Prime Minister of Great Britain, on a 'shoot to kill' mission. Terrible things were happening: torture, people being burned alive – you name it. On the night before the infamous All-Ireland Football Final Michael Collins virtually wiped out the English Intelligence, together with their informers, girlfriends and other associates in various parts of Ireland.

The 'Tans' decided to enact their revenge the next day at the match – opening fire indiscriminately on the crowd, killing fourteen people and injuring hundreds. One of the Tipperary players, a man called Hogan, was among the victims and the stand named after him is still there today. It was not called Bloody Sunday for nothing. To illustrate the atmosphere prevalent at the time, let us read the account of an address made to the Royal Irish Constabulary in Listowel, County Limerick, by Lieutenant Colonel Bruce

Smith, who was Divisional Commissioner for the Province of Munster. It is hard to believe his words, uttered on 19th June, 1920, but the exact text as follows was printed in one of the newspapers at the time.

> Well men, I have something to tell you, something which I am sure you would not want your wives to hear. Sinn Fein has had all the sport up to the present and we are going to have it now. We must take the offensive and beat Sinn Fein at their own game, martial law applying to all Ireland to come into operation immediately. In fact we are to have our scheme of amalgamation completed on 21st June. I am promised as many troops from England as I require, thousands are coming in daily. If a police barracks is burned, or if the barracks already occupied is not suitable, then the best house in the locality is to be commandeered and the occupants thrown out into the gutter. Let them lie there, the more the merrier. Police and military will patrol the county at least five times a week. They are not to confine themselves to main roads but make across the country, and when civilians are approaching shout 'Up hands'. Should the order not be obeyed at once, shoot and shoot to kill. If the persons carry their hands in their pockets, or are in any way suspicious looking, shoot them down. You may make mistakes occasionally, and innocent persons might be shot, but that cannot be helped and you are bound to get the right person sometime. The more you shoot the better I shall like you and I assure you that nobody, no policemen, will get into trouble for shooting a man. Hunger strikers will be allowed to die in gaol, the more the merrier. Some of them have already died, and a damn bad job they were not all allowed to die. As a matter of fact

some of them have already been dealt with in a manner their friends will never know about. An emigrant ship left an Irish port bound for a foreign one lately, with a lot of Sinn Feiners on board. I assure you men it will never reach port. We want you to carry out this scheme and wipe out Sinn Fein – any man not prepared to do this is a hindrance and had better leave the job at once.

This cost Bruce Smith his life because he was shot by the IRA later that summer.

The crop sown by Lloyd George at that time was to yield a terrible harvest, even to this day, and it was into this scenario I was born seven years later. By this time Ireland had been separated into twenty-six counties, which were ninety-eight per cent Roman Catholic, and six counties known as Ulster, predominantly Protestant. They hated each other. Many Protestant families left Southern Ireland because of the belief held by the majority that anyone who went to a different church or who practised a different religion was *ipso facto* 'West Britain' and therefore disloyal to the cause of Irish freedom.

Why was my father at the match? No other reason than that he and a bunch of fellow students from Trinity College decided to go. In the midst of the pandemonium he found himself lined up with a number of others, by the Black and Tan auxiliaries, six of them to be exact, each with a revolver in his hand. 'Put your hands up you effing Fenians,' was the command, and of course the wise thing to do would have been to obey. Unfortunately, according to my father, most of those in front of him were the worse for drink, as was the poor chap beside him, who was not capable of carrying out the order. This annoyed the auxiliary to the extent that he struck the unfortunate man across the face with his revolver, which incensed my father so much that he lashed out and floored the offender. Every action has a reaction, and as he did this another soldier fired at him, undoubtedly intending to kill him. Fortunately the bullet just grazed his shoulder, leaving a nasty scar for the rest of his days.

Many hundreds were injured that day, and that indiscriminate action by the Black and Tans did much to fuel the bitterness and hatred which is still around today. Lloyd George was determined that Ireland should remain 'John Bull's other island'.

Despite everything my family didn't leave – we had nowhere to go anyway, and all my father's future was tied up in the family estate in County Longford. All the time the climate was getting worse, a civil war within the country, plus De Valera's untidy arrangement which led to an economic war with Britain. These things set the scene for when I became old enough to go to school, run messages or take the dog for a walk.

I was soon to discover these were very dangerous and hazardous missions. I quickly learned what a 'Prodie-Dog' was – just one of the many insults hurled at me every time I crossed the doorstep.

My mother would often ask, 'Where is it all going to end?' For me it was hell on earth, and there was no escape. We lived in a cul-de-sac, with no other Protestant children for miles around to call on for support. It seemed to me the enemy knew every time I ventured out, and were waiting for me. It became so bad that my mother went to the local Catholic priest, who said he could do nothing, and suggested that we emigrate.

'No one is going to run me out of my own country,' said my father, so we stayed!

One thing I learned the hard way was to look after myself and I always believed the Lord took notice of my predicament and gave me that 'little extra' which helped on many occasions. Provided there were not more than two or three against me, I could give as good as I got, but I did take some terrible beatings. It is interesting that years later, when I began to climb the ladder of sports achievements, many of my former enemies became my strongest supporters. Despite the broken bones and scars, many interesting developments were to take place later.

Having no friends means you have to learn to do things on your own. During the holidays I was despatched to my grandmother's place in the country, which gave me plenty of time to develop my skills in throwing stones, learning football tricks and participating in the Irish game called Bowling, which involved hurling a heavy metal ball along the local roads, sometimes for miles. Although I didn't realise it at the time, all this was helping me towards the pages of the record book, and certainly helped in another well-recorded event which happened to me when, aged ten, I was in the Wolf Cubs.

My mother had arranged for me to join, mainly I believe to meet some more Protestant children. The nearest pack was attached to our local church in the parish of Sandford, and carried the title '33rd Dublin'.

One of our big events was the Annual Provincial Cub Sports, which took place in a well known girls prep school near Donnybrook, County Dublin. I was picked for the event named 'Throwing the Cricket Ball', which took place on the hockey pitch. I can see it to this day, surrounded by white railings, newly painted, beyond which were well kept gardens and lawns and finally a red brick wall, which went round the whole of the school. On the pitch officials were marking where the various throws were landing, and one particular boy from 23rd Dublin had outdistanced all comers so far, by about ten to fifteen yards.

My mentor in all this was 'Akela'; she was head of our pack, and a tough little ex-international hockey player, who kept telling me to keep calm, and my turn would come.

Sure enough, after what seemed like an eternity, a voice announced through the megaphone, 'Next to go: Campbell, 33rd Dublin,' and a cricket ball was thrust into my hand. Let the *Irish Times* describe what happened next, because for some reason their reporter was keeping an eye on me.

> This small ten year old, dressed in white with a purple sash round his middle, stood up and threw the cricket ball. He had a lovely slow rhythmic movement which obviously hid some remarkable mechanism, because not only did the ball soar over the white railings, it continued to rise like a rocket and vanished right out over the boundary wall and into the road beyond. I walked it later and reckoned he must have thrown it around one hundred yards!

I suppose today an immediate drug test would be called for, but I became the 'Mighty Atom' with a picture in the main national newspaper, a copy of which hung in my mother's bedroom for the rest of her years. Needless to say the incident caused a stir among all present, but nothing like the stir when I arrived home without my good blue cub trousers. My little cup which I had won was ignored and I was despatched back to the ground to look for them. It was holiday time, the ground was locked, so I had to climb over the high gates. Alas, the trousers were nowhere to be seen. My reward was no supper and early to bed – so much for the Mighty Atom.

Two years later, 1939 again found me staying with my grandmother, and one particular day I was sitting in the company of the three old Murtagh brothers, all bachelors, who lived together in a cottage they rented from my family for two shillings and sixpence a week, or half a crown as it was known then. My father had given them a radio and it was from this I heard Neville Chamberlain declare, 'We are now at war with Germany.' The first utterance following this came from the oldest brother, Binnie – 'Dem Germans will take some beating' – how right he turned out to be.

The interior of their cottage could have come out of *Macbeth*. The roof was thatch, the windows tiny and it had not seen a cloth for many a year. There was an uneven earth floor with a number of holes in it where food was placed to feed the hens which wandered in and out at will, and in the middle was the fire, that never went out. Above the fire was a hole in the roof with a timber pot through which some of the smoke went out and, when it rained, through which a considerable quantity of water came in. The stools on which we sat had only three legs, so balance of a high degree was necessary.

We drank tea from an old black pot which again never left the fire. It just simmered away and occasionally water was added. If one of the old boys thought it was getting weak another handful of tea was thrown in – as my mother used to say, 'you could trot a mouse on it.' This tea, together with boiled potatoes (they ate up to twenty a day each) and a rough porridge mixture called 'stirabout' formed their main diet, but their prized possession was contained in a large whiskey bottle stored in the thatch.

This was 'poteen' – they told me it was Holy Water – a colourless brew distilled from potatoes, barley with some methylated spirits added. If you were not used to it it could blow your head off. They used to drink it in fresh milk. There was no furniture, curtains or anything so grand in their cottage, but I will always remember three things which hung on the wall. One was an old mirror with a 'Gold Flake' advertisement on it, which the brothers used for shaving, a routine performed once a week on Sundays before going to Mass. The other two were gems – two pictures, one of the Irish Prime Minister De Valera, the other the Pope. Both of these were framed in wooden lavatory seats.

My grandmother visited the brothers from time to time to bring home-made soda bread which they liked. Most of the visits were spent arguing, which they all seemed to enjoy, my grandmother in particular. She was a well known 'character' in the district and somewhat eccentric to boot as the following incident, one of many, will relate.

It happened one Christmas when the postman delivered a large parcel wrapped in brown paper and tied with sisal twine. 'What in heaven's name can this be?' was my mother's comment – which was quickly answered when she discovered it was a goose. It had been plucked, and pinned to its breast was a piece of paper, on which were written the words *'The inside is for your father.'*

'Now what's the stupid bitch up to?' demanded my mother, who could not stand the good lady, for a number of reasons which will emerge later. The inside of the goose had been cleaned out beforehand, and despite close examination we could find nothing. We all assumed she had forgotten to put in whatever she intended, and the bird was kept in a cool place until Christmas Day when it was stuffed and put in the oven.

My family, and some friends who had come in for pre-dinner drinks, were all chatting away when suddenly the whole house was rocked by an almighty explosion which blew the door off the oven, the glass out of the windows, and splattered the goose all around the kitchen. Absolute carnage. Subsequent investigation, including interrogation of my grandmother, revealed that she had stuck a bottle of poteen into the goose's neck, which is why we had missed it. She might as well have used a stick of dynamite because the heat of the oven turned the bottle into a bomb.

Life went on, the war continued, but it did not mean a great deal to me then. Sport was my hobby – it came easily and I enjoyed it. The boxing continued as instructed until one day the coach came to me and asked if I would like to box a three-minute exhibition with a recent flyweight champion of Europe. This was to take place during the school championships. Of course I said I would, and it was to provide one of the most eventful evenings ever witnessed in the school or anywhere else for that matter. The experts now realised I was different – but more about that later.

One of my great loves was cricket, which I played at school during the term, and at senior club level during the holidays. Again, this ability to hit the ball great distances and see it earlier than most batsmen gave much pleasure to the spectators and had quite the opposite effect on many bowlers, who did not like being belted around the place by this precocious young whippersnapper. I recall one particular game in the Phoenix Park, batting against the man who was without doubt Ireland's best and most famous bowler, and whom the experts had said was good enough to play for any country. That being so I hit him from one end of the ground to the other, and over the pavilion. I will always remember his remark, made whilst standing at the gate as I came through undefeated, 'You can take that smile off your face young man. I've been hit for more runs than that.'

With hindsight, I probably should not have replied as I did, but I heard myself saying, 'You may have been hit for more, but never so far!' He didn't speak to me for years afterwards.

The local cricket club which I joined was not far from my home. It was in a lovely location with the River Dodder flowing through at one end. The bank on the other side was a favourite grandstand for our supporters, among whom were many of those guys who a few years earlier had been hellbent on knocking the living daylights out of me. Like the following I was to have in golf in later years, all they wanted to see was some mighty hitting, particularly if the ball went into the river. Irish wit at sporting events has to be heard to be believed, but I think it is fair to say that the 'Prodie-Dog' had now become 'Good auld Campbell'. Hopefully some of the past was also forgotten.

My debut into Irish senior cricket came when I was still at school, against the most powerful side in the country, Leinster. Both teams were neck and neck and a big crowd always turned up. My mother, a great fan, was very excited and kept telling me I must be clean and tidy and go onto the field looking like a cricketer, so off I went with clean whites, shoes and socks, and a hair cut. My first shock came when I realised my dear mother had ironed the creases of my trousers the wrong way – side to side instead of back to front. Fortunately one of the team had a spare pair which saved the day for me. It must have been a good omen because we won thanks to my contribution with bat and ball. Afterwards their captain, a world-class cricketer and regarded as one of the best cover point fielders in the game, recalled my arrival at the crease.

> It was a vital stage of the match when this slight young man, about fifteen or sixteen years of age, came into bat. I remember the bat looked too heavy for him, so I decided to move in to intimidate him. This was a mistake. Bowling to him in this instance was one of our most experienced international bowlers, who had played on many occasions against the top teams in the world. The first delivery was picked up by this young man, and all I can say is I have never had a ball hit at me so hard in my life, and I've played against the best in the world. It nearly went through me, and I foolishly thought he couldn't possibly do it again – only he did, and on this occasion I got out of the way and retreated. The next two deliveries were

despatched onto the roofs of nearby houses outside the ground. The young man's name was Tommie Campbell.

I was on my way.

Chapter Two
Starting the Ascent

School – many things pass through our minds during this period of our education. You think, What is there to look forward to? We hear all sorts of things and receive plenty of advice. 'All successful people have an education,' and an educated person earns more!' These were some of the well-worn pearls of wisdom that may not be true today. There was one particular thing said to me by an elderly relative in my earlier years which I never forgot – he said, in that wonderful slow Dublin accent, 'Whatever you do, always get a diploma to show you are good at it.'

One of the issues constantly addressed was what to do when you leave school. My mother had fixed views on this as far as I was concerned, and her main priority was for me to be a gentleman above all else. 'Always stand up when a lady enters the room, don't speak until you are spoken to, always raise your cap to the neighbours (this of course applied only if they were Protestants), and be kind to dumb animals.'

I have used this latter edict of Mother's many times in those cases when I could have allowed myself to be provoked by some foolish or absurd comment from some of the two-legged animals I encountered. When asked why I did not retaliate my answer was, 'I was taught to be kind to dumb animals!'

For some reason I became the subject of attention from

our careers master at school, a rather flamboyant character given to a lot of arm-waving and theatrical gestures. Because of his appearance and shock of unruly hair we nicknamed him 'Beethoven'. He was prone to quote passages, frequently wrongly, from William Shakespeare, or 'the Bard' as he preferred to call him. This was to show off his prowess at oration and acting ability, after which he expected us to name the origin of the passage, who said it, where and when. I remember after one of his favourite pieces... 'Friends, Romans, countrymen...' one of the class declared that it had been spoken by Napoleon. This extracted a loud bellow from Beethoven.

'What do you mean?' he shrieked.

'Surely you've heard of Napoleon, sir, he was the emperor of France,' was the reply.

Beethoven was not ready for this, because he could lose it very easily and one had to make allowances for this fact. Not only that, we were also all agreed that the lift 'did not go up the full distance', but to give credit where it is due Beethoven managed to restrain himself, and after a perceptive silence replied in a more dignified manner, 'You are an utter fool – your lack of knowledge stands out like a sore thumb – and what in God's name you will grow up to be is a mystery.'

One thing you learn in Ireland is that the inevitable never happens but the unexpected occurs constantly. Suddenly Beethoven's finger was pointing at me. 'What do you want to be when you grow up, Campbell?'

It was a question I was not really expecting, but I gave the answer implanted in my mind by my mother, 'A gentleman, sir.' This clearly took him by surprise, as indeed it did the rest of the class.

'Well now, isn't that interesting; this calls for a cup of sustenance.' This was always followed by, 'Any chance we could have one?' He always kept a flask of coffee on his desk, which we all knew was strongly laced with some powerful alcoholic beverage. We also knew he was very 'fond of a drop'.

After a good slug of 'coffee' he carried on, 'A gentleman, a gentleman. I wonder what you have in mind – can you give me an example of someone, apart from yourself of course, who might fit the bill?'

A shout from the back of the class, 'Someone just like you, sir!' came from a boy who sat alongside another character known as 'Meaty', because his father was a butcher. A big red-faced lad, Meaty was known to frequently utter only one word, which he did on this occasion with gusto, 'Bollocks!'

This of course drew attention away from me momentarily, as Beethoven commanded, 'Stand up whoever said that!'

There were twenty-six of us and at least half replied, 'Said what, sir?' and Meaty got away with it. The sound of the bell for the end of the lesson put paid to my giving any version of what a gentleman should be.

Coming back to Beethoven's original question, I really didn't know what I wanted to be. There was a war going on which had to be won or lost. The man with the little moustache was sweeping all before him. 'What will happen when he comes over here?' was a frequently asked question. I don't think the fact that Ireland was neutral would have made the slightest difference. One thing which could have changed the whole course of history as far as these islands are concerned would have been De Valera's acceptance of an offer made by Winston Churchill. This was the hand-over of a thirty-two county Ireland to the Irish people in return for Britain being able to use the treaty ports for their shipping. These were huge inlets which could hide the whole British Fleet, strategically placed as far as the Atlantic was concerned, but old 'Dev' refused, and as

I write this book all kinds of disruption, bombings and killings are taking place which would have been confined to the pages of history had some common sense prevailed at that time. Nobody seems to know when there will ever be a solution – as far as I am concerned there is only one, which is a dignified withdrawal by Britain from Northern Ireland and let the people there sort the problems out for themselves. Most of those to whom I have spoken to in England don't understand the Irish question, and really don't want to – an attitude which is quite understandable – it is costing the country a fortune. Withdrawal would be a three-day wonder, and people would ask, 'Why did we not do that a long time ago?'

Back to my schooldays; they were acceptable as long as you were within the jurisdiction and protection of all the school's facilities. Once outside that 'ring of confidence' you could not help feeling insecure. Looking back on the situation the sense of insecurity was accompanied by bouts of despair, although I did not really understand this at the time. It is in a lot of Irish people even today, and one does not have to scratch too deep to find it, despite the fact that on the surface they are a very happy and gregarious people.

Segregated schools were a major factor. They were institutions designed at that time in Ireland to breed active dislike and ill-will towards Catholics or Protestants, whichever was the case. It didn't just happen during my time, the seed was sown many years before. Going to and from school became a hazardous business because there was no one to ferry me back and forth unlike today, where large numbers of children seem to be continually chauffeured by their mothers, causing untold obstructions outside schools, and creating a rather overweight and un-streetwise school population.

Segregation of course went beyond schools and I can remember distinctly my surprise in later years at funerals of

Protestants seeing their Catholic friends standing outside the church because they were not allowed to go in. These were grown-up educated men and women, but that was the way, no variation, and indeed they often on occasions apologised for the fact that it was outside their control. There was one story told about a woman who got caught in a very heavy downpour with her daughter, and took shelter in a Protestant church without realising what it was. On discovering the fact she made her daughter swear that she would never tell anybody they had been inside a Protestant church because otherwise, to use her own words, 'they would be ex-communicated.'

In my day you quickly became streetwise, and two vital things you learned were the ability to look after yourself and to run like the wind. If you didn't, the consequences and exposure to bodily harm were very real. In fact it became so bad my mother had to set up a series of 'safe houses' along my route into which I could bunk if all else failed. This created more and more stress, and even I thought on occasions, *What a terrible way to grow up.*

However, life had to go on, and I took my education seriously – or maybe it would be more honest to say that I did where it involved the subjects I liked. Some of them – in particular algebra and maths – always presented problems. Indeed my father who, being an engineer and very good at maths could never understand this discrepancy, said to me one evening when I was struggling that I would be better counting the cattle in the field behind our home. On the whole though, my work was not too bad, and I did fairly well. Sport was a great interest and I enjoyed it. In fact, I did most of the normal things that lads do at school, and could sum it all up as a mainly happy and relatively uneventful experience. That is, until one day the school sergeant, genially known as 'Frosty', who always wore his war medals, came into one of my classes and, as he did with everybody, barked at me in a broad Glaswegian accent, 'Be in the gym at lunch break, the coach wants to see you.'

Johnny was the man, and I could not help wondering why he should want to see me. I was soon to find out. On entering his office I was greeted by the words, 'Sit down, I want to have a chat with you. How would you like to box an exhibition during the School Championships next month?' This was totally unexpected bearing in mind that three years earlier I had been barred from competitive boxing at the school due to the possible damage I might inflict. I also learned the headmaster had given permission provided that it was okay with me.

I quickly understood why this consent had been given. The other person with whom I was expected to share the ring was the ex-flyweight champion of Europe. My only remark in response to this news was, 'Is that the best you could get?'

Then I began to wonder all sorts of things, as one would, but I was snapped back to reality by Johnny's voice adding, 'There will be three three-minute rounds, you will be okay – he will go easy on you – he's a bit rusty because there are no overseas opponents due to the war.'

Then he asked me if I wanted to have a word with my parents, to which my reply was, 'What would I want to do that for – do you think I'm going to get killed?' The odds had always seemed to be against me, and this was no different, but I agreed to do it, reminding him that I hadn't had a fight for a long time, and would need all the help I could get.

Word spread like wildfire, and the wags had a field day with all the usual expected humorous ridicule, like, 'Jasus, Campbell, you're a brave man – do you think you'll go the three rounds?' One asked me if my opponent's mother would be there! He was referring to a certain time in my boxing past when my opponent's mother had waded into the ring and swiped me with her handbag for knocking out her son.

Despite all this I worked and trained very hard. Finally the big night arrived and I met the great man for the first time. His opening words were, 'Don't worry son, you'll be okay.'

In a situation like this all sorts of thoughts flash through your mind. *It's a big occasion, will I make a fool of myself in front of the whole school? Should I have said no at the beginning?* However, I recalled all those fights I had been through outside school with the odds against me, and made up my mind to give it the full twist whatever the consequences.

Before I knew it I was being escorted down the aisle between the many rows of gaping people, and climbing into my corner of the ring, where I sat down to tumultuous applause and encouragement from the assembled company. My seconds, one of whom was our coach, kept reassuring me that all would be well, and then above all this I heard the MC addressing the crowd with the words, 'Ladies and gentlemen, we bring you our special event of the evening – an exhibition bout between... consisting of three three-minute rounds.'

Then an eerie silence – I will never forget it – as if all this was a premonition of some sudden disaster.

The clang of the bell, followed by, 'Seconds out of the ring', brought me to my senses and the last words from my corner were, 'Watch that left of his', as I stood up and moved towards my man, who was already in the centre of the ring. It was not long before I felt that famous left of his on my jaw and quickly realised that evasive action was required otherwise I would end up with a very severe headache the following day.

Nothing very dramatic happened in the first round; my opponent was aware I had a punch which was something special and he was not going to take any chances, although I had no doubt he could have delivered me to the canvas had he so wished. However, that did not happen and when the bell sounded the end of the first round I went back to my corner feeling I had given a reasonable account of myself.

It seemed I had only just sat down when I was up again for the second round, and up I got again. Having decided I would try and put on a better show, it was not going too badly when my man decided he had better slow me down a bit and delivered quite a clip which knocked me back onto the ropes. We were approaching the end of the round, and as I came back off the ropes I spotted that he had dropped his guard and managed to one of my 'specials' flush on his jaw. I knew I had hurt him because he came in on me on the ropes, muttering, 'You little bugger – I'll kill you!'

But he hung on, and I knew if I could get another go at him I might knock him out. Mad thoughts for a young fellow of my age against a boxer of his calibre, but before I could do anything the bell went for the end of the round, and I found out later the timekeeper had hit it eighteen seconds early because the champ was looking the worse for wear. Bedlam had by now broken out in the hall.

Back in the corner my helpers acknowledged I had hit him with a good punch, but warned the next round could be tough for obvious reasons. This was borne out when I saw a different look in his eyes – he looked determined to teach me a lesson. I was managing to stand my ground quite well when along came another opportunity. This time I hit him under the heart, which really hurt him. Again he hung on in there and again they hit the bell early. Suddenly it was all over, I was still above the ground, not realising what had happened or what might be the consequences. I was soon to find out.

During tea afterwards, Jimmy the champ said to me that he could not recall ever having been hit harder by anyone in his career and it had felt, to quote his own words, 'as if you had plaster of Paris inside your gloves.' I learned afterwards this was a trick some fighters used – dipping the bandages they wore inside their gloves in the substance.

'Would you like to take up boxing seriously?' He added, 'I could always arrange a visit to my club and you can have a chat with the manager.' Once I had agreed, I soon found myself discussing the matter in the gym of that famous establishment, which boasted a full-size ring and all the other training aids which were part and parcel of such a famous club. All around the walls were pictures, including one of a famous Irish heavyweight champion called Jack Doyle.

I met him later; he was a tall, good-looking fellow who was at one time a contender for the heavyweight boxing championship of the world. He had many claims to fame, one of which was that he owned three hundred and sixty-six suits – one for every day of the year including leap years! A lover of wine, women and song, he had a good voice, and indeed when he was down on his luck in later years he would sing for pints of Guinness. Unfortunately, this got the better of him and it was a great pity to witness the decline, like so many others before him, of this great man.

He became involved with the wife of a famous American car magnate, and then married a film star called Movita. I can recall the wedding in Dublin, thousands turned out to see the event, which was quite hilarious. They spent the first few nights of their honeymoon in a hotel by the sea just outside Dublin, which was a mistake. All the kids in the area found out and gathered outside shouting 'Good old Jack', 'Give us a song', 'You're the greatest'. In the end the only way he could get any peace to continue his bedroom activities was to hurl a handful of small change out of the window, but this was quickly gathered up and the same old routine started up again. In the end it became so bad the police were called in to clear the area.

The marriage of course did not last, and I believe Movita's father gave Jack a payoff to get lost. He then took up wrestling and I remember going to see him fight, if that's the right word, another former heavyweight boxer called 'Two Ton Tony' in an open-air event at Dalymount Park, a famous football ground where Ireland played their international matches. They arrived hours late and in the first round both of them fell out of the ring during some kind of grapple, never to return. They were both the worse for wear, having been boozing all afternoon – it was hilarious. In the end, to pacify the crowd Jack got into the ring, with a lot of assistance, and sung *The Wild Colonial Boy* very badly indeed. So came and went Jack Doyle: a great character, and known as Ireland's horizontal heavyweight.

However, back to me and my boxing future. I was sitting in the manager's office, having sparred one full round with each of three selected opponents of his choice. 'Now Tommie,' he began, 'you are one of the most exciting prospects ever to come in here, and I am going to give you the best advice I know. Don't take up boxing – leave it out.'

His reasons for this amazing statement were soon explained. 'You are punching so hard now, what will you be like in a few years time? Lethal! You could cause serious damage to an opponent, and that would be disastrous.'

So that was that – I never boxed again, though I can't recall any great sense of disappointment at the time. I cast aside the boxing and concentrated on whatever else was available – football, cricket and another great love, table tennis. I saved up and bought myself a Barna bat which I still have, and practised every God-given moment, which nearly drove my mother mad. One of my routines was to hit the ball against a mirror on the dining room table. I don't know where I got the idea from but it seemed to help and improve my agility and speed around the table. I quickly began to make my mark, doing well in the championships against people much older than myself, with an ability to hit the ball very hard which was quickly noticed by some of the top people in the table tennis world.

It was also noticed by what was then known as the Church League and I remember being approached to know if I would play on one of their teams, because by so doing it would take them up into the First Division. This was something like the transfers we see today only there was no money attached but I said I would go along and look at their tables, hall and so forth and see what it was like.

On arrival I quickly came to the conclusion that this was a very High Church outfit. Waiting to greet me were some very intense looking ladies with no makeup on – indeed some of them had moustaches. I was introduced and asked to play an exhibition with their best person, which went by uneventfully and then the parson or curate came up to me and asked if I could spare a moment. I remember he was a young chap by the name of Derek, rather tall at over six feet, and we went across from this church hall into the vestry, where he said he understood that I was going to play in their team and become a member of the congregation. He then asked if I had taken the Lord Jesus Christ into my life.

I had never been asked that question before, and my reply was, 'Well, what did you have in mind?' He seemed to be somewhat nonplussed by this and started explaining that there were all sorts of extra-curricular activities which I could join in – he would be especially pleased to have my company when he went away for religious weekends.

I duly went home on my bicycle, which was my mode of conveyance in those days, and reported all this to my parents who promptly told me not to go back to that church. 'Because,' my mother said, 'that Derek sounds like a quare fellow.'

Religion can be very wearying, but for my part I can honestly say that I never attached any disproportionate weight to the views of my mother or anyone else. Religion in Ireland, like *apartheid*, is a lingering death. It has cost a great deal both in terms of money and lives lost, and the more the politicians seek a purely military solution, the worse it will become.

However, like everything else religion also has a humorous side. There is a story told about Mr Whalley, a very staunch Northern Ireland Protestant, who was on his death bed. The family were called together by his physician who declared that his patient may only have fifteen or twenty minutes to live, and wished to make a statement. The family gathered round the bed, whereupon the patient raised himself slowly and said, 'I want to tell all of you that I have become a Roman Catholic.' This news was received with horror by his family as they stood around him, and his daughter demanded, 'Dad, why in the name of God did you do that?'

The old man half rose and replied, 'Sure, isn't it better for one of them to go than one of us?'

Chapter Three

Swastikas in Dublin

Those who lived in Dublin pre-war were accustomed to seeing the swastika because it was actually the emblem of a large laundry which operated successfully at that time. It was situated quite close to Lansdowne Road, the home of the Irish Rugby Football Union, where our internationals are played, and outside the building was this large emblem which on reflection was the same as that used by Hitler, but of course the laundry had it long before him. All their vans carried this logo, and there was plenty of banter that Hitler had something to do with it, which of course was nonsense.

However, we also had smaller swastikas in evidence – these were worn by German 'sympathisers' which was probably understandable because many of them saw a German victory as a possible solution to the Irish problem. My dear mother used to frequently state that Dublin was full of spies, which was possibly correct seeing that it was a neutral zone, and I remember asking her one day, in my innocence, 'How can you spot one of these people?' I always remember her answer was, 'You never can son, because they're always in disguise.'

On the other side, apart from the swastika wearers, a lot of young people from the Republic of Ireland went and joined the British forces, and a large number of them died, including one of my sister's boyfriends. Another feature of life during the war was a certain gentleman by the name of

Lord Haw-Haw who used to broadcast on a wavelength which was receivable in Dublin and the rest of Ireland. Indeed I can remember hearing him on occasions and now and again he would make references to Dublin and what was going to happen in Ireland. I'm sure in retrospect a lot of people listened to him for some light relief. He was of course Irish, and at the end of the war he was captured and paid the ultimate penalty along with many others in that regime.

I also remember a German boy at school with me; he was a very nice chap and none of us bothered very much about him, indeed I can't remember anyone holding any grudge against him, nor did he against us. Life continued with many humorous incidents and some not so humorous. People were very confined – you could not travel outside the country – and with petrol rationing and that sort of thing it was even difficult to move about inside the country.

On that note I can recall getting my first inter-provincial place on the table tennis team which involved travelling south to Cork by train. We left the railway station in Dublin at just before nine o'clock in the morning and arrived in Cork at round about fifteen minutes past twelve that night. How we ever reached the place was a mystery – in several cases we had to get out of the train when it was going up an incline because it could not build up enough steam and power with the timber it was forced to use instead of coal.

All in all it was a memorable event. We played all sorts of card games and lost and won back the little money we had several times. We were young and able to take it, and the excitement of playing in your first big game was always there. Another feature was the taking on of the timber at certain stages on the route. For some reason the wood had not been kept under cover and was wet, which didn't help the overall situation, and in fact the train drivers used to say they had to bring the logs to the boil before they could get them to burn!

One event which made a big difference to our lives was the death of my grandmother in 1942. She was my father's mother, and he was an only child. She lived with her second husband, a retired naval commander, on various farms or estates situated in County Longford, which is more or less in the centre of Ireland. She was never a great favourite of my mother, who on regular occasions would exhort my father to go down and make sure she had made her will. This was because my father spent quite a lot of time and his money on these farms, mechanising them, installing electricity which came through a wind-charger as they were called then, and it was certainly Father's intention to spend the rest of his life farming when the old lady died.

Die she did, but unfortunately for the family she died intestate which of course meant that she had not made any will consequently all her estate went to her second husband. This character never did a stroke of work on the farms, and spent his time walking round with a gun and a dog, or riding horses, the type that would generally be referred to in Dublin at the time as 'a waster'. When the news broke my mother realised that what she had always feared had happened. She and my father went down to the funeral in County Longford, and as was the case in those days the mourners who came were treated to refreshments of one sort or another, be it alcoholic beverages or tea and cakes. I remember Mother saying that she couldn't even get a cloth for the tea table because the man had everything locked away, and quite a battle ensued before she could make the table look decent. My father foolishly contested the whole situation in court, which only cost a lot more money since he had no chance of getting anything. We lost what had been the general lifeline of the family, and also the chance of any more holidays down on the farm.

I had learned many things during the early holidays there. It was lonely because there were not a lot of other children around – it was rather a remote part of the country. I vividly remember an old gentleman, who lived in one of my grandmother's cottages on the farm, died and before he was actually certified dead all the locals knew that there would be a wake. In those days this had to be seen to be believed because it turned out to be one massive booze-up that could go on for days and days, with professional mourners and 'friends' of the family who were really only there for one thing.

When poor old McGuinness was on his deathbed in the little cottage I used to go down with my grandmother and some of the servants. There would be people knocking on the window and shouting through the door 'Is he dead yet?' – their only interest being when the festivities would begin!

One of the main things that had to be available was a drink known as porter, which was a sort of low-priced Guinness. They drank quantities of this and also large bottles of poteen – an illegal substance brewed close by – plus of course plenty of whiskey. This particular wake went on for two or three days, with bodies lying around all over the place. During these festivities the corpse was laid out on the bed with four candles round it, two at the head of the bed and two at the foot. All the blinds were drawn and the whole thing was very eerie. People would go in and wish the deceased well, and I remember one old lady who was absolutely mad with drink came in and said she had distinctly heard the angels' wings flapping over his head. My grandmother said this was absolute nonsense and it was probably just the blinds blowing gently at the windows. This sort of repartee was part and parcel of wakes such as this, which were typical of rural life throughout all of

Ireland.

My grandmother was quite a lady. She loved the good life and wore flamboyant clothes, with big hats and parasols. There were always parties going on in the house, and musicians would come in and play into the small hours and the old lady always stayed with the festivities until the very end. She loved jewellery and had plenty of it – some of which was very valuable. She had also won third prize in the Irish Sweep at one time, so all in all her husband received a very good haul, but within six or nine months he had sold everything up because local opinion was not very favourable towards him.

Another memory of my grandmother was going with her in the horse and trap into the nearest town, Longford. It was only about seven miles, but seemed like an eternity. The horse she used, a lovely chestnut, was called Jessie and the road on which we had to travel was quite hilly, so poor old Jessie would have to go down to a slow walk now and again. One of the features of the trip was Jessie breaking wind but one became used to that. Later on the memory of those trips came back to me when a story was told about the then lady prime minister who came to meet her counterpart in Dublin, whom she didn't particularly like. He had arranged for the two of them to travel to Dublin Castle along this route in a lovely coach drawn by two grey horses. It so happened that it was a very warm day, and halfway along the journey one of the horses broke wind in a very loud fashion. This was followed by a perceptible silence in the carriage which was finally broken by the Irish prime minister who turned to his guest and said, 'I'm very sorry about that, please accept my apologies,' to which her reply was, 'I shouldn't worry, because if you hadn't said anything I would have assumed it was the horse.'

Chapter Four
Work and Some Play

'I knew that old bitch would not make a will – you should have made her do it,' was the tone of a conversation between my mother and father following the demise of my dear old grandmother who, as mentioned earlier, had died intestate leaving everything to her second husband. I mention this because the implications as far as I was concerned soon became very clear. It was obvious that all our worldly wealth at that time and for the future had been wrapped up in the family estates in the country, and now there was a distinct shortage of cash which was going to have a disastrous effect on my further education. In a few words this meant that I would now have to go out to work.

There was an immediate offer on hand to go into a business owned by one of our relations. This was a large multistore in Dublin into which I could make my way as an apprentice and work through the business with the promise of a crock of gold at the end of it. The fact that this idea didn't appeal to me at all did not go down very well with the family. I was not afraid of the hard work which would have been involved – I just could not see myself in that role.

My refusal to go along with the plan rather left me in limbo, and the fact that I was not properly qualified to do anything did not make for an easy solution to the problem. Eventually an uncle of mine 'opened the door' for me to enter the raw wool business. Although I was very naive when I started, the education and experience which I received in that particular establishment set me in good stead all the rest of my life.

The owner of the company was a larger-than-life, very colourful character called Charlie who ruled the place with a rod of iron, punctuated with a very liberal helping of effing and blinding which I had not been used to at all beforehand, and so consequently it took me rather by surprise. In fact, the first instance of this was when I had to collect him to go to a dinner and on arriving at his very nice home I was greeted by his wife, a wonderful lady, and ushered into the lounge to await the great man. Whilst I was sitting there and making small talk with the lady of the house the air suddenly filled with a huge bellow from upstairs. 'Eileen, where's my effing stud?' I was probably the most embarrassed I had ever been in my life up to that point, but I soon came to learn that this was part and parcel of the man, and therefore also of the job, and I would just have to put up with it.

During the years I was with the company I had to learn the many thousands of different grades of wool. These then were subdivided into degrees of fineness contained in each particular fleece, which multiplied the numbers yet again. I also learned that the finest wool from the merino sheep, used for making the cloth for South American military uniforms, or one of the most expensive cloths in the world used for billiard tables, can only be reared in very dry countries such as Australia or South Africa. Also that the coarseness in wool for such things as carpets could only come from wetter conditions, like those in this country.

I learned all these things and became quite proficient in them. After a while the salesman instinct started to stir inside me and this, allied to a sense of urgency within me to do well, was for me the beginnings of my whole future business career. Many things during that period set my standards for later years. One was the fact that I had to be in work at six o'clock in the morning, which meant leaving home on my bicycle at half past four. I can honestly say that I was never late during the whole time I was there, and I have carried on that tradition throughout my whole life. When I started in selling as the great man's assistant, I was never allowed to refer to any notes when we were talking about various lots and showing samples. This created within me a wonderful memory for numbers and figures which stood me in good stead for all time.

They were tough, rough years but there were many happy times and many funny times, particularly associated with the boss and the collection of men he had working there. Among them were some real Dublin characters, most of whom were possessed with the spontaneous wit which is the hallmark of Irish humour, and all of whom had felt the wrath of Charlie's tongue.

One old chap called Joe Fish suddenly appeared beside me one day wearing the startled look which he always had on his face. 'Tommie,' he said, 'I think I should tell you the Boss spoke to me this morning.'

'Fine,' said I, 'and what did he say?'

Back came the answer, 'Get out of my effing way!'

We had a lady telephonist, Molly, who was a rather rotund and excitable spinster and referred to by Charlie as 'the fat lady'. When Charlie was on the rampage round the office effing and blinding right, left and centre, dear old Molly used to cross herself and cry, 'Jesus Mary and Joseph does he know he's committing a mortal sin?' She was genuinely concerned by this trait in Charlie's nature, and horrified by the language which abounded in the place.

The office wasn't very large, with only one washroom shared by male and female alike. Most days Molly needed to visit the Washroom on a number of occasions, probably for a quick puff since smoking was not allowed openly in the office. Her absence from the telephone on those occasions irritated Charlie, who, when wanting to be put through to a number would yell, 'Where's the fat lady?' knowing that she was in the washroom which was close by her switchboard. Then he would 'rush' the door of the washroom as if he wanted to go in, give it a good kick, and yell, 'Is anybody in there? Hurry up!'

This Fred Karno atmosphere prevailed throughout the whole day, and as long as you weren't on the receiving end it was 'better than the Abbey' as we used to say.

Charlie also had a brother whom he had taken into the business under sufferance after his own business venture failed, a fact which Charlie reminded him about practically every day of his life. Harry was a complete opposite to Charlie, a much quieter character who muttered a lot under his breath. When Charlie was doing his daily rounds of the warehouse where the wool was processed he would charge about, and out of the corner of his eye would spot where Harry was. Then would come the roar, 'Where's my effing brother?' to the acute embarrassment of poor old Harry, who would have to endure similar ridicule all day long. Another favourite trick of Charlie's was to buzz the phone for Harry, then just as he picked it up he would hang up, shouting, 'That effing brother of mine! Never at the phone when I want him!'

Jobs were very scarce in those days and there was no trade union within the company so people put up with a lot and worked for very low wages. In fact when I started off I was given the princely sum of twenty-five shillings per week, and the arrangement at home was that I had to give half of this to my mother, leaving me with twelve shillings and sixpence to do all that I wanted to do. I remember when I received my first wage packet I went to see a movie in a funny old cinema called The Stella in Dublin. I had one of the cheapest seats, which cost sixpence, and I was shown to my place somewhere up in the gods by an usherette – a difficult task since the war was on and batteries for torches were very scarce. Because of the shape of the cinema the number of seats in each row decreased as they got nearer to the front of the auditorium, and as the usherette showed me to my row she switched off the torch. Not realising that the rows had changed in length I reached out to – as I thought – put my seat down. There was no seat there, and instead I grabbed a lady's leg; she let out a loud screech and when the usherette arrived to see what all the fuss was about, the lady claimed I had assaulted her. Needless to say this was far removed from the truth, but she also had a rather substantial boyfriend with her and I had visions of receiving bodily harm. Fortunately, common sense prevailed and everyone calmed down, but as a result I shall never forget the spending of the first money I had ever earned.

I got on very well with Charlie, because I was working the best part of twenty hours in a day, here there and everywhere. I took to the business like a duck to water, and one day Charlie decided it was time I tried, some selling. This I did, and if I do say so myself I was good at it. One of the main attractions of the set-up was an agreement that I would receive a commission on any sales which I effected. This being so I launched myself into it with gusto, since I could see the pound signs coming up before my eyes, and with them the knowledge that all the little bits and pieces that I wanted to buy were coming within my grasp.

I went all over the place, lugging with me my heavy suitcases loaded with all the various samples of wool. I spent countless hours sitting in railway stations, waiting for buses, and when I started off going away for more than one day Charlie informed me that I was to be sure that I found reasonably priced hotels. Also he made me a member of an organisation called the Commercial Travellers Association which entitled its members to a ten per cent reduction in certain establishments. I can clearly recall setting off on a 'world tour' of Ireland by bus, train and Shanks's mare, and arriving in this little place called Kilkenny (famous for its cats) late at night, absolutely worn out, and it was the first time I had ever stayed at a hotel. At about quarter past eleven at night I lugged my cases through, and faced the grumpy old character sitting behind the reception desk smoking a cigarette. I remembered Charlie's instructions about not staying in four-star hotels, and indeed this one would have struggled to make one star, so I approached the desk with apprehension. I can distinctly remember my first words, which were, 'Excuse me sir, have you any low terms for commercial travellers?'

The old chap just looked up and replied, 'Yes, f... off!' If anybody was ever to ask me how I would describe a feeling of despair, that was it.

However, he must have taken pity on me because he followed up his initial remark by saying that although they didn't have any room at his hotel I could try across the street at Mrs Cassidy's – she took in the hotel's overflow now and again. She turned out to be a nice old lady who gave me a room about four flights up, and once my head touched the pillow I remembered little else about my first night away as a commercial traveller.

These are just some of the memories of my introduction into the great commercial world, and I often look back and reminisce with a certain amount of pride and achievement because a great many young men of that time would have just thrown in their hat and not carried it through.

In later years I rarely talked about these beginnings, but on odd occasions when I did talk about it to younger people the response was, 'You bloody fool, I would never have put up with all that; you must have been out of your mind!' However, I know that all the things that happened to me in those early days made me the equal of anyone in my field and I really was able to run rings round most of them because I was never afraid of hard work. The traits of my character which were formed at that time were to see me through many hours of need and dark times.

I worked every hour of every God-given day selling, and even at that tender age I created a whole new department, with Charlie's permission. I started to bring in wools from overseas, and was the first to introduce them into our market; at the same time I could see my commission growing steadily ready to provide me with a new cricket bat, clothes or even a little holiday. The actual payments, however, were not taking place. I asked the accounts office if I could please have my commission for the past three months or whatever, at which I was told I would have to get clearance from the Boss. This clearance unfortunately never came.

At the time I didn't realise it, but that was to be one of the most important moments of my life. The bottom line was that the great man let me down very badly and wouldn't pay me my commission, which absolutely broke my heart. I went home to my parents and told them that all my hard work had been to no avail. My mother, who was never short of a few words, declared that she would get my father 'to go in and see the old bastard', but that never happened because my father didn't think it would be the right thing to do. I made my mind up that I would not stay with the company, but would try and use my sales ability for my own ends. I therefore left Charlie's establishment, and to say he was not best pleased was certainly an understatement, because I had certainly made him a lot of money and opened up a whole new field for him with the overseas wool. He knew that I was a worker and a loyal one at that.

Anyway, I started off with a partner who had been a

former customer, and had to suffer many insults from my former employer because I was starting up as a competitor to his own business. He even sent out notes to the wool dealers stating that any price I offered he would better, and also to the customers, saying that anything I offered for sale he would sell to them for less. Needless to say all this made it very difficult for me, added to the fact that the man with whom I had gone into partnership turned out to be a crook. I found myself in even deeper water, all on my own, trying to fend off the great Charlie on the one hand and on the other cope with the things which my partner had done without telling me. In the end the background experience I had already gained stood me in good stead and I never gave up, but just ploughed on and sorted everything out, until finally I came out with my own company on an even keel with a reputation for good service and good delivery that was second to none anywhere in the world.

On three occasions in America I won the Best Carpet Wool Supplier award from the committee of supervisors, and that gave me a lot of satisfaction. The path to those awards had not been easy, but given the chance to live my life again I would not flunk those years, because they set me up and gave me a built-in immunity to anything else that might happen. Time is a great healer and as the years passed Charlie relented and we became very good friends. He carried on in his rough and wonderful way, and lived to a ripe old age. I bore him no malice, since in my experiences with him the pluses most definitely outweighed the minuses.

In between Charlie's ranting and raving, and being told to 'f... off' by hotel clerks, I did manage to play some sport, which included football, cricket and table tennis – in fact anything that had a ball attached to it. There were good times and not so good times – it was not easy to get time off for these events whilst I was working for Charlie. I remember one occasion when my team reached the final of the

Provincial Cup in cricket; it was an all-day match, and because of this I was not allowed to play in it, to my horror, and instead was despatched to do some job in another part of Ireland. This was one of the great disappointments of my young life, since I was a key figure in the team, and the rest of the players couldn't understand the situation – most of them thought I should have left work and played in the match regardless. It wasn't much fun, that's for sure.

However, one occasion which was fun was when we won the Provincial Championship and were celebrating on the Saturday evening. Transport was non-existent because of the war, but one of our number worked for the Dublin Tramway Company. He was pretty high up within the company, which meant that he had the key to the tram 'stable' as it was called, which was not very far away from the pub where we were all supping our Guinness. Without more ado he led us all off to the big tram shed, well after twelve o'clock at night and before we knew it he had taken out one of the trams. We all piled aboard and went off on a jaunt into Dublin, and even though I had consumed a vast amount of Guinness I can remember the startled look on the faces of those out that late at night, when they were passed by a tram full of rather jolly and exuberant young cricketers.

At that time there were certain establishments where you could get a drink after hours, and we parked the tram outside one of these and went in through the back door. We hadn't been there very long when the police came along, having been alerted by people ringing up and telling them about a bunch of lunatics driving a tram, followed by more calls about a tram with nobody in it, parked outside a pub in a well-known part of Dublin. It all ended up quite reasonably I think, but the awful part about it was that Gerry was fired from his job with the tram company, which I suppose was to be expected under the circumstances.

There were many other wonderful instances which could go down in the folklore of cricket. I remember another very tense final when we were playing just outside Dublin at a lovely ground packed with people. Two members of our team had not been able to get there due to a transport breakdown. The captain of the side was a well-known Dublin bookie, and again like my old friend Charlie, every sentence of his was punctuated by effing and blinding, and because of the missing players we had to bring on a Dublin magistrate called Tom who was probably one of the worst cricketers I have ever seen. I recall at an absolutely crucial stage of the match – one of the opposing team hit an absolute dolly to Tom, and of course he dropped it. The captain, Joe the bookie, from a distance of about twenty yards and in front of all the crowds of people bellowed out, 'F... you Tom!' It was such an anticlimax, and I remember I just rolled over with laughter as a stunned silence hit the crowd, followed by roars of laughter as people saw the funny side of it.

The humour was there, as it was with another memorable incident involving our friend Tom. Having won the championship the winning team was invited to play at a private cricket ground set in one of the most picturesque parts of Ireland. It was owned by a well-known colonel whose family had built it and called it The Oval. One of his pride and joys was to invite famous cricketers to play in his team and many famous names accepted his offer.

The game was always preceded the night before by a dinner at which refreshments flowed freely and of course our intake was in excess of what it should have been, bearing in mind we had this important game, next day.

We paid the price and the first problem arose when one of our opening batsmen was too ill to leave the pavilion and I was instructed to take his place. This was a new experience for me – being a bowler I was accustomed to appearing later in the batting order. However, I was in better shape than the others.

Amongst the colonel's stars was one of the Australian fast bowlers who was taking things seriously and going through us like a dose of salts.

It was so bad with only one more man to come in and less than twenty on the board that the captain was forced to eject the not so well opening batsman, a very nice chap called Des, on to the pitch but this did not work. He managed about twenty paces, maybe the fresh air was too much for him, but ended up violently ill. We had a crisis.

Our captain approached his counterpart on the field, which of course was the colonel, and asked for a short time-out to see if he could find a replacement. Little did he know the person in mind was making advances to his wife behind the building!

The first thing was to disengage him from the amorous interlude which was achieved quickly, only to find he was very much the worse for drink. 'For God's sake, Tom, get your ass out on to that wicket and see if can add a few more runs,' was the message.

By some miracle I was still 'in' and could watch this drama going on. Finally, Tom appeared weaving his way towards me like a feather in the wind, immaculately attired as always in his silk cap and cravat. I don't think he really had the first idea of what was happening.

I should add that Tom, apart from being a popular and nice chap, was without doubt the worst cricketer I had ever seen; he just was without a clue, but that added even more spice to what was about to take place.

I walked out to meet him and was met by two loud wind noises, one from his rear, the other from his mouth, followed by, 'Is the wicket taking spin dear boy?' It should be said our Australian friend was not amused by all this but more was to come.

'Don't worry about me, I will keep my end you, you get the runs.' In as diplomatic a way as possible I escorted him to the crease with the words, 'Tom, put your bat in that hole and pray!' The spectators knew what was happening and gales of laughter were rolling on to the pitch but all this stopped as our man started his fifteen-yard run and launched this missile at Tom.

He didn't move and I am convinced to this day that he never saw the ball, which flew past him to the wicket keeper's gloves. A great roar went up from the crowd, suitably acknowledged by Tom.

Now it was time for the next delivery. I shall never forget what happened. The Australian came pounding in and I must add he was a very quick bowler by any standards, certainly faster than anything we had ever seen. Just as he was about to deliver the ball Tom took a hop step and jump up to the wicket and with one finger raised, issued the command: '*Stop.*'

It stunned everyone, including me; the bowler glared at him and said, 'What's up cobber?' to which Tom put on a lovely little smile and issued the now famous words, '*A shade faster please!*'

It was certainly one of the funniest moments ever on a cricket pitch. To his credit the bowler saw the funny side and took it back to Australia where it now holds a place in their book about famous moments in cricket. The end came soon after but it was a day to remember. Sadly, Tom is no longer with us but his memory lives on.

The captain of a great team which we had for about two years was a wonderful old chap (anyone over twenty-one was old to me in those days). Jack was a wicket keeper and if you made any error on the field you heard a great roar from behind the stumps. One of the team was a great tall man, about six feet six, who wore glasses and looked like an absent-minded professor. He didn't really seem to grasp the ways of the club and the etiquette on the field, but because of this great height he had the ability to bowl very fast without really knowing where the ball was going! He only ever made the first team on one occasion – a game at a lovely little cricket field outside Dublin which is now a housing estate, unfortunately.

At a vital stage in the game Jack decided he would bring on the 'Bomber' as the tall chap was known. Bomber was over the moon at the chance to bowl for the club in senior cricket and everything else went out of the window. The only thing in his mind was to go back the required distance and bowl the ball at the batsman. While Bomber was walking back Jack was arranging what he thought were the best fielding positions for him, when suddenly without any warning Bomber launched the ball a full toss totally out of control – and hit Jack full belt in the chest. I shall never forget it! 'Christ!' was the only word Jack could gasp as he sunk to the ground, completely pole-axed. It took him quite a while to recover, and he looked up at Bomber who was anxiously leaning over him and demanded, 'You bloody clown – what did you go and do that for?'

Work was one of the contributing factors to my ending what the press and all the pundits said was the beginning of a very promising career in cricket. I also had an offer to join the professional ranks as a member of the ground staff – an offer which my father was absolutely dead against, remarking that I should end up drawing white lines round the boundary! Once I had made my decision not to let my work suffer in favour of cricket I never played competitively again, which on looking back was probably a stupid decision but one which I made and stuck with, nevertheless.

Chapter Five

Go It Alone

The disappointment of not receiving my commission from Charlie certainly burned a hole inside me, and I had come to the realisation that whatever I did in that organisation I would always have problems. Unfortunately, I had nobody to turn to. I did have a good father and mother but neither of them were what one might call 'commercial animals' any more than I was, so basically any decisions which I made – some good and some bad – were made by me. Looking back I often wish I had had access at that time to some sound advice because I was full of good ideas but did not have the business acumen to carry them through to the success they could have achieved. Or to put it another way, to the success they achieved for others.

I didn't have a great deal of money, which was why I elected to go into partnership with the gentleman I described in the last chapter. He promised me the Earth, money to finance the business and the premises and all associated with that, in addition to assistance with marketing. Armed with these good intentions I set forth into the great big world of commerce full of high hopes. In retrospect I quickly found out why so many businesses fail at an early stage when enthusiastic young people like me start off. There is no substitute for doing your homework which of course you never feel is necessary at the time.

It would certainly have helped me to have done mine,

because my partner did not live up to my expectations; he left me high and dry with no money. I also found he had without my knowledge sold a lot of wool to various people at ridiculously low prices, and I did not know what to do. In the end what I did do was stay the course and found ways and means to carry on. I got rid of the 'bad apple' and brought in some good people and started laying the foundations for what was to become an international and well-known business.

In the midst of all this turmoil I got married. I met the lady who is still my wife today at a table tennis club, and not too long afterwards I made one of the better decisions of my life. My decision was not approved by many around me – we were both too young, my business was not established – but I always remember a good friend of mine at that time saying, 'If you wait until you can afford to get married then you never will!'

The reverend who performed the ceremony was a good friend of ours, and one memory which has stayed with me was of the rehearsal on the day before the wedding which was attended by Kate and I, a few close relations and the people who would be assisting at the ceremony. Everything was going along fine – 'Do this, do that, kneel here, say this, say that, and then when the ceremony is over we will go into the vestry and you will sign the book and hand over the licence and...' At that point the vicar must have noticed that a strange look had come over my face, not to mention that it had also changed colour. 'You do have the licence Tommie, don't you?' I had to put my hand on my heart and say that not only had I not thought of it, but I never even knew I needed one. There we were one day away from the wedding, and short of something which normally took several weeks to obtain. To make matters worse the look on my future father-in-law's face showed clearly that he was wondering what sort of idiot his daughter was marrying.

However, my father-in-law – who was known as DJ – was without doubt one of the most wonderful people I have ever met in my life. He was absolutely straightforward and would go across the world for you, so he was determined that something would have to be done, and quickly! For my part I was in a state of shock and was only brought out of it by the reverend saying that we would have to go and see about a special licence right away.

It was now late on Friday afternoon with the wedding due to take place the next day, and the offices for special licences were all closed. We had to set off and find the home of the man who had the power to do something for us. After a lot of hurtling round the highways and byways of suburban Dublin we found his home, and we found him. To say he was not amused was putting it mildly. To say that by the time we got to him he had taken in quite a lot of alcohol was also a fact, and at one particular stage I could see no way of overcoming these two problems. Yet again the patience and endurance of my friend succeeded in getting the necessary piece of paper which would enable us to go to the next stage and obtain the special licence. Many hours later, and ten pounds poorer, we had the necessary licence which allowed the ceremony to go ahead. Some time later when my friend the reverend and his wife were having dinner with us, he confided that if we had not succeeded in getting the special licence he would have married us anyway.

It was the beginning of a very happy marriage and Kate has always been a tower of strength to me. She was her father's daughter with a very similar outlook on life, which was very good for me because it straightened out a number of idiosyncrasies which I had accumulated, and which I was well rid of. We were fortunate in being able to buy our first home – a lovely bungalow situated in a beautiful suburb of Dublin – and we were to remain in that area for many years surrounded by good friends with whom we had many happy times.

'Someone has to pay the rent' was an expression deeply imprinted in my mind and it was a well-known one in Ireland. In rural areas there were, even then, situations whereby small farmers kept their pig inside the house, and he was known as 'the man who pays the rent.' In those dwellings the windows were hardly ever opened, and the aroma was something you would not smell in a chemist's shop! However, having taken the steps towards going it alone I quickly found out several things, among which was the fact that the word 'Irish' absolutely stank among those in the wool markets. This was a direct result of sharp practice amongst certain exporters who got up to all kinds of tricks.

One of these was to top up the bales of wool with very nice material so that anyone examining them would think they were getting a prime product, but once they took the first layer off the rest of the contents were nothing like the top, and indeed I saw instances of this in different parts of the world. In most cases the unsuspecting importer had paid for the goods in advance and found that he had no comeback. This sort of thing was totally foreign to me; I had my own ideas and made up my mind that I was going to do things my way. That was the start of a crusade round the world with one aim: to establish a situation whereby any wool which Tommie Campbell shipped to anybody was correct. Building up this reputation was a long haul and cost a lot of money because it had to be taken in stages, but by sheer doggedness I did achieve it and became recognised as one of the best providers of carpet wool in the business.

I was very proud of my reputation and this did not go unnoticed by the press and various other people, but little did I know that in the years ahead my own government would try to smash all this, and in the process ruin my life.

I learned that buying wool was a great art, a very interesting study of people, and I became very good at it. Within Ireland I can safely say I visited every town and met hoards of people, from fascinating characters with homes up in the mountains to titled ladies and gentlemen who lived in castles.

In the beginning and throughout all this I had to cope with the 'gunfire' from my previous employer who, as I have already mentioned, had sent the word out that whenever I bid for some wool he would pay more, and this severely stretched my limited resources. One of the interesting aspects of the wool buying which I came across was that many a farmer depended mainly on the money he received for his fleeces after the sheep had been shorn, and the actual sale of those was a major event in his calendar. If they knew I was coming to buy their wool a very pleasant and sincere little ritual would take place. When the wool deal had been done I was taken into the parlour where there was a table set for me, and the most favoured fare was a boiled egg. I don't know how many boiled eggs I ate during those days but I think I could have had another entry into the *Guinness Book of Records*! No way could you possibly turn down this great event, and you always sat alone – the other good people would sit around and chat and watch you eat.

On the other side was the character who would produce a bottle of whiskey and insist you partook of a large quantity of the contents – his main idea being to get you sloshed so that you would pay him more money than the wool was worth. These were all tricks of the trade, because a lot of the buyers were unscrupulous and tried to screw the unfortunate wool growers so they had to resort to tactics of their own. These included dampening the wool to get more weight into it and when the fleece had been rolled up all sorts of different things were placed inside to increase the weight; I had quite a museum of articles which had been discovered over a period of years.

After a while the trade realised that I meant business and I was accepted. Charlie and the others realised that it was costing them a lot of money to carry on the regime of offering more money than I did because I had found ways and means to make this have a boomerang effect on them, with the net result that I was allowed to live in comparative peace. Of course, whilst it's very important that 'well bought is half sold' I had to set about selling all these different products, which involved me in extensive travel around the world.

I was away on average six or seven months in every year by train, boat or plane, and there were some very interesting episodes during my travels. I met a number of famous people – like the time in New York when I was the guest of Jack Dempsey who had a famous bar there. He was a great character and treated me well, especially when he heard that I had done a little boxing, though we never got into a ring together as he was a little past it by then. He had had a sad life financially, and I remember a sign up in his establishment declared 'Jack Dempsey, the pugilistic idol of all time'. He certainly was a great man.

Another time, in 1955 to be exact, when I was going to America on the *Queen Elizabeth* we set off rather rapidly from Southampton with a somewhat depleted staff due to a pending strike by the crew. I was standing on the deck looking across to a meeting being held on the dockside by a number of them, when suddenly the captain decided it was time to up and away, and the ship pulled out, leaving the rest of the crew shaking their fists and shouting after us.

Our first stop was Cherbourg where we took on some passengers. I was going up the steps on the promenade deck when I noticed two gentlemen coming down. I was prepared to give way and showed signs of doing so when a voice said, 'Come along, come along.' As I reached the top of the steps I realised that the speaker was a very familiar character in a grey felt hat, none other than Mr Molotov the Russian foreign minister. Beside him was an enormous gent who must have been six feet tall, obviously his body guard, and as stepped off the gangway I said, 'Thank you very much Mr Molotov.'

'Oh,' he said, 'you recognise me then? Where do you come from and where are you going?'

The result of this was that I struck up quite a nice association with him which carried on for the rest of the voyage. He was on his way to the Prime Ministers' Conference in San Francisco and we had some very interesting conversations together. He had quite a big staff with him who were in the rooms over his state room, amid great security, and I was the only one of the passengers invited to the private cocktail party which he gave for them.

I shall never forget it; they were a very interesting body of people, some Russian, some Poles, plus many other nationalities, all absolutely subservient to the great man for whom they were working. The drinking aspect of the party was quite remarkable, since the only alcohol consumed was Russian vodka which was much different to anything else I had tasted before or after. There was a toastmaster there and every so often he would give a toast to Mr Molotov then everybody had to take up their drink and down it in one gulp. The net result of all this was that I finally swayed to my table for dinner certainly the worse for wear but with the realisation that I had been privileged to meet and talk with one of the world's most interesting characters.

I was particularly fascinated by his knowledge of Ireland, but then he had been the Russian ambassador to the court of St James, and spoke perfect English. He knew all about the Northern Ireland question, he also knew about the fact that Winston Churchill had offered a thirty-two county

Ireland to De Valera in return for using the ports. I asked him what in his opinion was the solution to the particular Irish question and he said, 'There is only one way to do it. Britain will have to finally get out of it and leave the people to sort out the question for themselves.' I did not elaborate on the matter, bearing in mind all the countries the Russians had taken over with their own doctrine.

Each day we met and had a chat, mostly pleasantries, and struck up what could be loosely termed a happy relationship. All the time the other members of my table, who incidentally were all Jewish, were most anxious to try and meet the great man and say round their tables that they had met Molotov. On our final day when I was having a chat with him I spied one of the members of the table coming towards me. He was a small gentleman, a New York lawyer, and I thought, *Hello, here we go*. He came right up to the three of us and said, 'Good morning Mr Molotov, I hope I am not disturbing you. We Americans are just a bunch of kids and we want peace – why won't you give it to us?'

There was a perceptive silence and a faint smile flickered across Molotov's face as he gave his answer, which was simply, 'I don't believe you.' At that moment he turned, said, 'Goodbye Tommie,' and went off with his huge bodyguard.

The little New York lawyer turned his startled face to me and said, 'Do you think I got through to him?'

Another thing I shall always remember were Molotov's steely blue eyes – the coldest eyes I have ever seen. His smile never reached his eyes, and when he spoke to the lawyer they were like cold diamonds in the snow. We finally arrived in New York and a tender came out to meet the ship, full of American reporters – and a more raucous bunch you never would meet. There must have been some prior arrangement because Molotov was going back on this particular boat with all these media people, his staff and an enormous quantity of luggage. I was there when he left and shook hands with him. Next thing he was sitting on a pile of suitcases – one of the media people had stuck a stetson hat on his head – and as the tender moved away from the boat he turned and waved to me. 'Take care of yourself Tommie – give my love to Ireland.'

One of the pluses of travelling round the world is the people you meet. On that particular trip I had been working very hard, and decided to go out from my New York hotel to a place called the Latin Quarter to have something to eat. On arrival there the guy in charge of allocation of tables informed me that all the tables were full. There was another gentleman who had come in at the same time and was standing just behind me, and there was a sudden change of attitude. A table for two was found and we were asked if we would care to share it – we agreed and sat down. He turned out to be the Spanish ambassador to the United States and in the course of our conversation he told me that before that he had been the Spanish ambassador to the Argentines and one of the missions he had to perform was escorting Eva Peron to meet the president of his country, General Franco. His description of the lady and the vast quantity of clothes which she had taken with her was quite fascinating. It occupied a few hours of what turned out to be a very pleasant evening. One of the things he mentioned about Eva Peron was that she had expressed great disappointment at not being invited to meet the queen of England.

Life went on apace and the wool business progressed satisfactorily. I had managed to overcome the vagrancies of the Irish market and was proud to have played a major part in re-establishing the quality of Irish wool in the world markets. However, I decided I would like to get nearer the sharp end and move up from the raw materials into manufacturing with the final wish to one day be actually selling to the public. The reason for this was that I examined the margins for the various stages put onto the product and the nearer you got to Mr and Mrs Smith buying a carpet in the High Street, the wider and bigger the margin on the finished product. The mark-up by some of the stores on carpet was quite ridiculous, and in my opinion unnecessary.

At this particular time it took months and months to get a carpet – if you wanted it down by Christmas you virtually had to order it the previous September, and had to put up with the autocratic attitude in the shops. There was no real service, they closed at half past five, and this started a chain of ideas in my head that I was to put into practice at a later date – 'Why don't we have late night opening and a supermarket type facility for people to buy carpets?' I was also convinced at that time that I could introduce what I called an 'impulse buy' into carpets – in other words if the scene and atmosphere were right, and the selection good, it would spur on people to buy something that really was locked away in the back of their minds.

At this point, in the mid fifties, I was involved in a survey the terms of which were to find out what percentage of all the rooms in the United Kingdom had a carpet; the answer came out as seven per cent. This immediately showed me the vast market which was available, and at that time when I was down in the southern states of America I learned about a little old lady in a place called Chattanooga who was making bathmats from cotton on a funny little machine which she had made. I went to see her and her machine, which just made row after row of cotton pile and produced very nice bath mats. Immediately it went through my mind that this method could be used to make carpets, which until then were all made on what were called Axminister and Wilton looms, a very slow and costly process.

To cut a long story short, I attacked this idea of mine and everyone I spoke to thought I was mad, including the boss of one huge man-made fibre producer from whom I had asked for a special length of fibre to spin yarn for this process. I can clearly remember what he said to me, 'You're wasting your time young man, this will never be used for carpets and I suggest you go home and look after your business.'

They were all wrong – that process grew and grew into what is known today as tufted carpeting, and certainly in excess of eighty per cent of all the carpets made in the world are made by that process. It transformed the town of Dalton in Georgia from a small hick town into a booming carpet centre. It also transformed mechanics into millionaires and I was privy to watching all this and see one individual, whom I had advised to go into the business, become a multi-millionaire. He was also a golf nut, and announced that he would pay any golf professional one million dollars if they could legitimately get his handicap down from sixteen to single figures, but nobody ever succeeded in doing so.

Back home I met another remarkable character, initially by accident. One day I had arranged to have lunch with the governor of our leading bank corporation who was a good friend of mine, and we had agreed to meet at a then very famous restaurant in Dublin called Jammets. I remember midmorning on that particular day Willie rang me up and asked if I minded someone else joining us for lunch. When we arrived there I met this little man called Cyril Lord who, as I am sure many people will remember, changed the whole face of the carpet industry. I can safely say that I have never met a person quite like him. He was no respecter of people or tradition or anything else, as was obvious at the lunch.

Jammets was then one of the most respected restaurants

in Europe, and Monsieur Jammet was a friend of mine and lived close by my home. Once we were seated in the restaurant one of the first things Cyril Lord asked was, 'How long does it take you to cook a steak in this establishment?'

Monsieur Jammet was quite taken aback by this and said, 'Well, it depends how you would like it sir, but about fifteen or twenty minutes.'

'Balls!' said Lord, 'in my restaurant (the Pig and Chicken in Northern Ireland) I can cook steaks and have them on the table in five or six minutes.' Eventually, after the whole meal had gone along in this vein, we rose to leave and as we reached the door Jammet took me to one side and begged me, 'Never to bring anyone like that here again.'

I went to see the great Cyril in his gigantic plant near Donaghadee. As you walked through the place a jingle which had been made by the Beatles came on at intervals throughout the day – 'This is the carpet you can afford – by Cyril Lord.' He also had a TV advertisement with Batman dressed in suitable gear coming in through the window of a New York skyscraper. The two guys in the room turn to each other and one says, 'Who's that coming in through the window?' The other replies, 'It's Mr Matman!'

Lord was also a very competent water-skier, and every Sunday he would go down to the harbour at Donaghadee which would be full of people out for walks. He would give an exhibition to the crowds, who paid particular attention in the fervent hope that he would fall off. However, he never did, and as he came up out of the water he would turn to the crowd and give them a two-finger salute to show that he knew what they had been thinking. Like many others before him, his business failed, but in his time he certainly set the world on fire and if he had been prudent enough to install the proper management in his organisation there would have been no limits to his achievements.

Having been involved in the beginnings of tufted carpets, I then in the mid sixties finally started the first cash and carry carpet business in the world. They were very interesting days and of course I had no idea then just what the future consequences would be. This idea changed the whole carpet industry – think of the thousands of carpet shops there are today and the millions of homes which have wall-to-wall carpet made on the tufted principal.

There was one other side to it which arose from the fact that I had to spin a special yarn in the early days for these tufted carpets. I took myself off to Northern Ireland where there was an available amount of flax-spinning machinery which of course had been used to make linen. I got my hands on some of this machinery and converted it to do the job required, but one of the mistakes I made was not patenting the machine I had invented because it was refined and modernised in the years to follow and became one of the major units in the process.

I was frequently in Northern Ireland and made a lot of friends there, and business connections. In the plant where we were spinning the yarn there were three and a half thousand people and in the plant where the machinery was being made there were seven and a half thousand people, and out of those eleven thousand there was not one Roman Catholic.

Being a Southern Irish 'Prod' I was acceptable but it did give me a very clear insight into the whole situation, and confirmed to me that for fifty years nobody had done a damn thing about the problem either from the North or from the South and a lot of people, politicians included, were making fortunes out of that line which was called The Border.

I was to be reminded in years to come when I visited

South Africa that a similar situation existed there but there too, nobody was trying to bring the two factions together or resolve the problem.

Chapter Six

The Gathering Storm

It was late in the evening when the phone rang at my home. I recognised the voice at the other end immediately as being my senior counsel and I also immediately detected a chilling urgency in his tone.

'Tommie, listen carefully. The manager of the dye house has just been found dead in one of the vats. Do not answer the phone after you have spoken to me, or speak to anybody until I find out more about it.'

What did all this have to do with me? To give an answer I have to go back to the beginning.

In Ireland, home industries at that time were very vibrant and active, particularly in the more underdeveloped areas of the west and north-west, where a woman could knit a pair of men's socks in an evening, and many of the crofters had hand-looms in their homes where they wove rough cloth which was then sent to a finishing mill for export all over the world.

The actual manufacturing unit which carried out the finishing and made yarns and materials of its own was owned by the government, and as such was governed by their rules and regulations. At that time we were developing all sorts of wools to suit their manufacturing purposes because Irish Tweed was rapidly becoming famous throughout the world, due to its quality and design.

The items which were to have spectacular success were

the white sweaters and cardigans called *bawneens*, and in order to make these the actual yarn used had to be, to quote the manager's own words, 'as white as the driven snow'. This raised some problems with him and he called me in one day and told me that he wanted me to make him up a quality of wool with no discoloration whatsoever, but as far as he was concerned there was a snag.

'Tommie you understand our buying regulations as far as wool buying is concerned. We are only allowed to purchase standard qualities as quoted on the world markets for obvious reasons, the main one being the board can check my prices anytime to see if I am competitive. For these new lines I must have pure white wool none of which is listed under the standard qualities. The better ones of these contain approximately eighty per cent pure white, the balance being yellow and therefore no use to me.

The only avenue open to me is to purchase the standard type and sort out anything that is not pure white. To do this I must have skilled sorters but there are none in our employ because there is not enough permanent work nor would they wish to live up here in the wilds of Donegal.

Therefore this is what I want you to do:

a) Sell us the agreed standard type that will contain the highest quantity of white wool.
b) Invoice this to us in accordance with our laid down contract conditions, e.g. the actual weight you receive into your warehouse at so much per lb. We will pay you on this invoice.
c) You will then take this consignment to your expert wool sorters and remove whatever is necessary to ensure we only receive white wool.
d) We will pay you the standard sorting rate on the weight of wool sent for sorting.

e) You will keep a record of everything extracted and send it for sale by public auction at the Dublin Wool Sales, in our name so the cheque will come into out account.

Standard practice in the wool business but to someone not conversant with the contract conditions it could be said you invoiced one weight and delivered another. On the other hand the proof was always there for anyone to see. As we were dealing with a government department they were treated like the police, everything face up on the table. The manager, James Redington was one of the straightest people you would ever meet, he accepted no gifts from anyone nor was he offered any, certainly not by us. The hypocrisy, pretence and skulduggery that was to follow formed the basis of one of Ireland's most dramatic law cases culminating with my company being charged with twenty-three counts of fraud against a government organisation. All this had stemmed from a dramatic announcement by the opposition minister who announced in the Irish House of Parliament that he had irrefutable proof of a large scale fraud etc., etc. He was of course saying all this under privilege and I found out it was us.

Looking back in retrospect, which of course I did not know at the time, it transpired that a high official of the government wool manufacturing industry had been taking out the opposition shadow minister's sister much against his wishes. He then jilted her which caused a lot of bad feeling which erupted when the two met in a pub at some official gathering in the West of Ireland. As often happens in Ireland a fight started and the opposition minister came off second best. So when someone came along with these false allegations to him he saw the opportunity to get his own back without ever trying to check out their validity beforehand. This was a man who later rose to be a High Court judge but more to the point this was politics at its most sordid, mean, despicable circumstances. He and his cronies I am sure never gave a thought about who might be hurt so long as they achieved their aims.

The Fianna Fail government which was in power had no alternative due to the publicity but to hand the matter over to the proper authorities. I found out later that they knew there was no foundation to the charges and reckoned they would backfire against the opposition because they knew I would never be involved in this type of carry on. In fact they apologised when it was all over but that was no good to me at the time.

It was only a matter of time before the police arrived on the scene to go through all our records, this went on for nearly a year driven by the opposition no doubt. They went everywhere interviewing all kinds of people and the superintendent in charge was one of the nastiest pieces of work I have ever encountered.

There was never any question of trying to find out what actually happened, they did not ask on one occasion. They would not show their evidence, it was then I realised I was being set up and if I did not look after myself the consequences could be serious. So I said to myself, *right Tommie, time to counter attack.*

Our company lawyers at the time were a well known firm called A. & L. Goodbody and I would like to once again place on record that they were superb. We decided to appoint as our senior counsel one of the most famous names in this area of criminal justice, Sean Hooper. This was the nucleus of my team, I shuddered to think of the cost particularly in the knowledge that even if I won there was no chance of getting one penny back. The battle was on and you have to live through such a trauma to understand the emotional shock not only to you but all your family, friends, business associates, not forgetting those who will always say 'so that's how he got his money' and words to that effect. Because of the media coverage nothing was left out.

As expected I was formally charged, the gloves were off. I had to appear in court, my fingerprints were taken and I swore then that someone would pay for this. I should also add amongst my greatest allies in all this were my competitors and friends in the trade, they stood by me all the way.

On the first day the court was packed, I was sitting with my legal team, the press were there in force sensing something dramatic would unfold. I would like to point out these proceedings were to establish whether or not there was sufficient evidence for the judge to send me for trial. He would hear the case for the prosecution followed by our defence.

The former went in to bat calling various witnesses and then for the first time I began to put together what had happened.

Books and documents were produced that had been stolen from our premises; nobody had mentioned these at any time. In the main they were showing the weights of the white wool despatched which of course were less than the original weight invoiced for the reasons already set out. The prosecution also said they had been received anonymously through the post to the minister's home.

It did not take me long to work out which books they were or that they measured two feet by eighteen inches thereby making it impossible to fit through the letterbox. To make sure I checked this out knowing where he lived. It also confirmed the person who had taken them, a nasty individual who used to work for us. We found out subsequently that they had been delivered by him and he was in collusion with the minister. Unfortunately we never got the opening to prove all this in court, neither did his name ever come out.

I might add in conjunction with my senior counsel that I

had spent hours working out technical questions, every evening I would go over everything. I think I averaged three to six hours sleep at best. It paid dividends because we were hammering the prosecution at every stage in our cross examination and I could not wait to get this minister into the witness box because my counsel and I had vowed to destroy him. There was a long way to go before it was his turn and my network was getting the message that he was looking for a way out. The press were also beginning to sense all was not well and had moved over to my side, but we never let up or eased the pressure.

Then a terrible thing happened, the dye house manager in the Donegal mill was found dead in one of his dye vats. He was a good man, efficient at his job, straight as a dye and would have been on of the main witnesses in our defence. He suffered from a bad asthmatic condition and always carried an inhaler which he used frequently. The verdict was suicide but questions were asked as to why his inhaler was never found, the vats would have been empty because it was a holiday weekend, we will never know.

After ten days the senior counsel for the state created a bombshell by throwing in the towel. He realised as an ambitious man that he was not doing his reputation any good. He probably did the right thing because later he was to become attorney general. We could now see events moving our way and the prosecution's case was only halfway through. It was also obvious that the judge was becoming restless.

Finally we came to the manager, who was first of all examined by the state prosecuting counsel, then when it came to our turn I had to present my counsel with all the questions and the answers which would be appropriate. We spent hours and hours going over our defence, and it was a great tribute to him that he was able to absorb the whole thing. To hear him cross-examining one would think that he was a highly skilled textile expert.

The manager was in the witness box for over two days and the whole story unfolded. He confirmed everything we had said. He also thanked us for all the things we had done for them in research and development, for which we had not expected any payment. He also put it that my company had been instrumental in the huge international success of their products. It was at this point that the state decided they had had enough, and after twenty-odd days they threw in the towel.

After all the anxiety and tribulation it was a great relief, but it was also a bitter disappointment to me because I wanted to see those who had perpetrated the charges in the witness box. I think it was with this in mind that the state decided to withdraw, although they said afterwards they too would liked to have seen the perpetrators shown up in their true colours.

I was given a public apology; the state mumbled on about their evidence and that they had been misled, otherwise they would not have proceeded. This was a load of nonsense. As I had mentioned time and time again they had many opportunities to ask the right questions and they would have received the right answers.

The costs involved were enormous, tens of thousands of pounds, none of which was recoverable, and I came to the conclusion very quickly that pursuing this was only putting good money after bad. I would just have to grin and bear it and get it back by sheer hard work in the business. I was called in by those at the highest level of government, who said, 'We knew you would clear yourself – sorry to put you to so much trouble.'

I remember walking down the steps from the Houses of Parliament in Dublin and thinking 'Well, bugger you! You put me, my family and my whole business through this nightmare for over two years and that's all I get from it.'

However, I did find out afterwards that the whole process was steeped in politics – it had cost one good man his life – and I made up my mind that in future I would try not to get involved in any other good deeds and treat all government departments *et al* the same as I would the police. From those days nearly thirty years ago I have often watched various trials and cases and seen people come up for retrial after they had been wrongly and unjustly prosecuted, and thought to myself, *Well, I'm not surprised, because some of the tactics employed make a travesty of the maintenance of right and justice.*

What transpired afterwards was what one would expect. My family, and in particular my mother who was very upset, were relieved that it had finished the way it had. So many people took the chance to say, 'Good old Tommie, we knew there was nothing to all this.' In point of fact, many of them were hoping I would be put behind bars, because one of the things I discovered was that in Ireland success in your own lifetime can be a double-edged sword.

My business recovered and picked up. I did not allow the proceedings to get to me and burn away my confidence, as can so often happen. All my friends in the trade were very good to me and gave a wonderful party at the end of it all. I should also add that during the trial I had been elected president of the Irish Wool Federation, and having to make a speech at the annual dinner in the midst of all the goings-on was not the easiest task I have had to perform. I got by and succeeded in reaffirming the confidence all our customers and friends worldwide had shown in us from the beginning. It was now time to move on to other and greater things.

Chapter Seven
The Hereafter

I found myself being appointed onto various state boards; I suppose the government did feel some obligation towards me after what had happened, and it was fair to say that we were on good terms. Life continued within the business and I took steps to tighten up as necessary in order to protect ourselves wherever it was commercially possible. I appointed one of our brightest young men to the whole stock control which had previously been the domain of the character who had endeavoured to bury us.

The new man was a very bright young chap who was due to get married shortly, and I remember him saying to me one day that he was going with his fiancée on a trip to Rome, which included a semi-private audience with the Pope. When he returned I said, 'Well Dick, how did you get on? Did you enjoy your visit to the Vatican?' at which a look of horror came over his face.

'Well sir, we had a very distressing and awkward occurrence during the audience.'

It transpired that they had stood in a row and His Holiness came along with one of his assistants. Jane, Dick's fiancée, thought it would be a good idea to ask His Holiness to bless their engagement ring. As the great man came along Dick held the ring out in his hand. In a few moments the Pope was facing him and smiled, looked at the ring and gave a nod to his assistant standing alongside.

The assistant took the ring and popped it into a bag he was carrying – the assumption being that the ring was being offered as a gift! The Pope moved on, leaving the unfortunate couple standing there. They couldn't run after him and ask for the ring back, so they asked their tour guide, who felt it would be very difficult. In fact they never got it back, so it turned out to be an expensive, heart-rending experience, but no one could ever have anticipated something like that happening!

Life is full of surprises and one day I was summoned again to the government buildings to meet the head of the government who had me in for a cup of tea, over which he said, 'Tommie, how would you like to lead an unofficial delegation to Eastern Europe?' The year was 1962 and at that time the Irish government did not recognise or have a relationship with any of the communist countries, but at the same time they realised that they were huge potential markets, and this was where I came in.

Naturally, I wanted to know what they had in mind, and the answer came back that in conjunction with the government I was to select a small team that would go to Czechoslovakia on the pretence of visiting the Brno Fair down near the Austrian border. It all sounded very exciting, so of course I agreed, and put together a team which included the editor of one of our best-known national newspapers, and a couple of others involved in agriculture and industry. We went by Czechoslovakian jet to Prague and one of the things I remember was that they were serving draught beer, and I had never had that on an aeroplane before. I might also mention that in the course of the preparation for this trip the minister had informed me that as far as they were concerned if we were caught or imprisoned they would refuse to know us. We were therefore entirely on our own and those were the conditions under which we went.

It all turned out to be very interesting because I had never been to Prague before and it was fascinating on this my first trip to a communist country to see the glory that must once have been. We stayed in a huge hotel that was very run down, no plugs in the handbasins, no soap in the bathrooms, but fortunately I had brought all those things along myself, including towels.

We were met at the airport by state officials, then a remarkable thing happened – we were all split up. I was staying on in Prague, but I had no idea where the others had gone, though I was informed they were going to see other departments and that we would meet again when we were going home. In the meantime I had no idea where they were and no means of communication.

It had been arranged for me to have dinner that evening with the president in Prague. It was one of the most remarkable meetings that I have ever had. Before I left my room I had set one or two of my belongings a certain way which would tell me later if they had been tampered with in any way, since it was impossible to lock the door. Indeed, when I returned later that evening it was obvious from the trap I had set that all my stuff had been gone through, which didn't surprise me at all – it was in keeping with the whole environment at that time.

In the meantime I met the president and a number of officials at a semi-state banquet which had been arranged for me. I will always remember that there was a small orchestra there and when I entered the room they proceeded to play *Danny Boy*. Unfortunately they played it very badly, but at least they made the effort. I had brought along various gifts which I had been told would be welcome, such as cigarettes, bottles of brandy and a couple of hams. I gave each of the chaps in the orchestra a packet of 'Craven A' cigarettes, and their faces lit up as if they had been handed the crown jewels – they couldn't thank me enough.

Eventually I sat down to dinner with the president and various other officials. At the beginning I thought that one of the people present had an Irish accent, and must therefore have had Irish origins. However, I discovered they had a school where they taught their people to speak English with certain dialects, no doubt all part of the great espionage scene that was going on in those days. It was quite uncanny to hear it, as indeed was their knowledge of the Irish question.

During dinner the president said to me, 'I want you to know you are free to go wherever you want and to ask me any question you wish.'

That being so my first question was, 'Mr President, why do, you have the cardinal as a prisoner in his own palace?'

To which the president replied, 'He must conform to the rules and regulations and not preach dissent and revolution. If he is prepared to stop this and abide by the laws of the country then he can go about freely without any hindrance.'

I then asked him various questions about religion and he said that people were able to practice their religion, and indeed I visited both Greek Orthodox and Roman Catholic churches while I was in Prague, but generally speaking the situation was as one would have expected. One other question I put to the president was, 'If this country is the great place you say it is, and there is freedom of movement, why do you have all the barbed wire round the frontiers, and machine guns to shoot anyone who tries to leave?'

His reply was, 'Our country is different to your country – in your country most people want to emigrate and you allow them to go, all the clever people, the intellectuals, whereas here in Czechoslovakia we believe they should stay in their own country and make it a better place for everyone to live in. That is why we do not let them out willingly – they have to apply for the proper papers and that is the way it is.'

No matter what question I asked they had a definite answer, indeed they were extremely well coached in how they should answer, and they all spoke perfect English.

We then got down to talking commerce and the president introduced me to the head buyers of their textile division who at that time were buying large quantities of wool from various parts of the world. They had no problem about dealing with us, the payment terms were an irrevocable letter of credit and I spent some time talking with these people and visiting them in their departments. The net result was that Eastern Europe became one of our largest and best export markets for wool products.

The time came when I was to be put on a plane to fly down to Brno to attend the fair and meet other dignitaries. I arrived at the airport in Prague and found myself on board this old plane which certainly looked as if it had been through the whole of World War Two. The tyres were very bare and the outside was screaming for a coat of paint. It was even worse when I got inside. I found myself seated next to the inside door – they were all hard seats, and when I went to put on my safety belt there was none to be found! As I sat there I watched all the people coming on board, many of them old folk with bags and bags of vegetables and all sorts of gear which they put on the open shelves above the seats. The noise was horrendous, and the smell was worse, and I thought, *God, if anything happens in this plane nobody knows I am on it, so it will be, 'Thomas Campbell – lost without trace'!* Indeed, something did happen.

It was a short flight from Prague to Brno, and we were only about twenty minutes out when the starboard engine caught fire. It was only a two-engined aircraft, and everybody started screaming. The pilot was making strenuous efforts to put the thing out but was not succeeding, so he decided he would have to fly at a tilt so that the flames coming from the engine would not set fire to the fuselage. He therefore went into a steep bank, which resulted in all the vegetables deluging down on top of the passengers and onto the floor. It was an inferno in the cabin, and it reinforced my view that this was really it, and that my last hour had come.

We flew the rest of the journey in that position, with flames belting out of the engine. Fortunately, we did not catch fire but the approach into Brno was a horrendous affair. We came in on one wheel, skidded all over the place, crashed into the wing of another aircraft and how the whole thing didn't go up in smoke I'll never know. Somehow or other – and all credit to the pilot for a miraculous landing – somebody up there was looking after us, and we managed to get out reasonably undamaged but mentally very shaken.

On arrival I was expecting to meet the rest of our party but there was no sign of them whatsoever and an official told me I was going by car to my hotel. The car was a great big old thing which had originated from the Skoda works in Czechoslovakia, and the driver decided to show me how fast it could go on the most dreadful roads. The journey only took about twenty minutes but it seemed nearly as bad as the air disaster, with this man going at breakneck speed and missing things by a whisker. All in all by the time I reached my hotel I was a nervous wreck. There was still no sign of any of my comrades.

The fair was interesting, and I will always remember that on display they had the actual spaceship in which Yuri Gagarin had gone into space – it was absolutely tiny. I sat in it and thought, *Just imagine being propelled into the atmosphere in this small 'utensil'*. Gagarin himself was there, and I saw that he was in fact a small fellow, otherwise he would really have had a problem! It was quite an honour to meet the man who had been first into space – the year of course being 1962.

They wanted me to share the room in my hotel with three other people – two Russians and a Pole – and of course I objected to this. Finally I managed to get the manager who spoke reasonable English. I told him it wasn't good enough and that I was a high-powered official from the Republic of Ireland etc., etc. It seemed to me that if I was going to get anywhere I would have to pay for it, so I told him quietly that if he found me a room on my own I would give him something. He wanted to know what it was but I refused to tell him until I had the room. In the end he told me to get the gift and meet him in the lift. We ended up in the lift, which was obviously the only safe place to negotiate and I gave him a tin of corned beef. This did the trick, because in no time I was ensconced in a lovely room facing across the square in Brno.

I quickly learned that this sort of carry-on was widespread throughout the whole of the Eastern Bloc, and on future trips I always went well-armed with suitable goodies which were worth their weight in gold. Later on when we invited the Czechs back to our country they were absolutely delighted and ate and drank everything that came their way. They were certainly not a regime that was as pure as the driven snow, but the people with whom we did business were very straightforward and honest. They always paid promptly and provided you delivered exactly what you said you would, there were no problems. The markets turned out to be very lucrative and we exported millions of pounds' worth of goods to them.

As a company we had built up a good relationship with the Czechs and because of this we did a lot of bartering with other countries throughout the world in return for some of their raw materials. The most difficult part of it was trying to get some of their natural products for barter, such as oil. They wanted to sell watches and clocks which they had made but which unfortunately were not very good, fountain pens and all sorts of bits and pieces. By and large it shows that where there is a will there is a way, and business can be done in the most difficult of circumstances.

I left that first trip to Eastern Europe a much wiser man, but I will always remember the feeling of despair in the places I visited. They all seemed to be grey and drab with soldiers everywhere and I just felt so lucky to live where I did. It takes something like that to make you appreciate what you have, and what other people have to put up with. Other memories include seeing a queue a couple of miles long in Moscow's Red Square, in sub-arctic conditions, waiting for ice-cream; going on my first boat trip on the Danube, to discover that it wasn't blue at all, but absolutely filthy; seeing the secret police breaking up a demonstration in Warsaw with ruthless efficiency. All these things become interwoven in the particular fabric of your being, and remain with you for the rest of your days.

The near air crash in Brno reminded me of another crash I was in, whereby on landing the front wheel of our aircraft caved in and we were lucky to bale out without any trouble. On another occasion, coming from Augusta into Atlanta in America, the pilot suddenly discovered the front wheel was not locking, so we had to circle for hours on a beautiful warm and sunny day. I remember looking out of the window and wondering if I was ever going to be on the ground again, whilst at the same time watching them getting the special crash gear onto the runway. The build-up of cars around the perimeter was enormous as people realised there was a drama going on and an aircraft in trouble. While all this was going on I was just sitting there waiting for something to happen, and in the end it was an anticlimax, because the front wheel did lock and everything was okay.

I had another incident in an old Wayfarer which caught fire on just a short trip across the Irish Sea, and the stewardess brought round whiskey for us. I didn't drink whiskey at the time, but I had half a tumbler full and didn't even taste it! On another flight from London to Brussels the plane I was in was struck seven times by lightning. They say lightning never strikes in the same place twice, but it strikes at the same person, because my plane from Johannesburg was also hit at one time, which threw the plane through the air as if it was nothing.

Not surprisingly, people thought I was a jinx and indeed for many years afterwards no one would fly with me because they said it was dangerous, but as I said to them, 'I'm still here!' Even so, I went through many periods when I feared flying and at one stage would put up any excuse not to fly and would go by train wherever possible. Finally I went to a doctor friend of mine, who told me I just had to do something about it. He said, 'Are you going to creep and crawl through the second half of your life? You've just told me you have to go to Bombay next week – go and get into that plane and get on with it!'

I remember well that my wife went with me on that trip. The plane was a DC10 and I suffered the agonies of the damned on take-off from Heathrow, but gradually my confidence came back and I stopped worrying about it.

Thankfully my flight from Brno back to Prague was less eventful, and when I went through customs into the waiting hall, there were my other colleagues. We exchanged notes, and they had had no more idea of my whereabouts than I of theirs. The newspaper chap wrote about the whole episode when we got back, and we were the forerunners for many further delegations; in due course there was recognition for these countries and what we did became very commonplace.

I must have made a reasonable job of that particular trip because I was then asked to undertake others. One which stands out in my mind involved me in organising a visit by the Irish prime minister to Mrs Gandhi in India. I shall always remember that great lady because she was certainly one of the most beautiful women I have ever seen: poised, articulate, striking, in fact, ten out of ten in every department. It was a most interesting and fascinating time.

Our prime minister was briefed by us about this and that, and one of the things we said to him was, 'Be very, very careful – you may be asked to drink some buffalo milk.' Because agriculture was such a big thing in Ireland, part of his itinerary included a visit to the particular factory which produced this drink. To my horror he consumed about a pint of the stuff, which had drastic repercussions on his stomach and he would say himself he spent one of the most uncomfortable times in his whole career trying to forestall the reactions of this liquid, in the middle of which he had to go and meet the Indian prime minister.

India, for those who have not been there, is a fascinating place. I attended one wedding to which there were fifty thousand guests. There were obvious examples of where the rich had got richer and the poor had got poorer, since they obtained their freedom, but then money has a habit of going that way. I found the people very interesting, and I actually met many of them. In particular the Hindu religion interested me, and I read a lot about it afterwards and found it quite fascinating. One of the facets is that a Hindu has two mothers – the one who gave birth and the sacred cow – and this is why they never kill the sacred cow, because it would be killing the mother. These cows roamed all over the place, eating vegetables which were badly needed for starving people. I saw on one visit, during a very bad drought, a whole family lying dead from starvation, and alongside them the holy cow, also dead. I thought at that time, in the mid to late sixties, that India was a smouldering giant ready to explode onto the commercial world, and that it could be a real competitor to Japan, but nothing like that happened until many years afterwards; even though the talent and ability were certainly there. They just didn't seem to be able to get it all together.

The Taj Mahal lives up to all its expectations – it took twenty-two thousand people twenty-two years to build – and it has to be seen to be believed. Walking in the streets around it was a real hazard, with small children begging and every conceivable stunt being performed to extract sympathy and money. I was staying with a well-known family and had the opportunity to meet their Maharishi. This chap was very famous and had just been helping the Beatles with certain problems which they had, and I spent a lot of time talking to him. In the course of conversation I mentioned my problems with flying and he said, 'You are just suffering from stress, and you don't know how to cope with it. With the number of miles you travel and the hours you work, you have got to be able to switch off.'

He then taught me, within a few days, what he called 'the death sleep'. I can safely say that this saved my sanity, if not my life, because it taught me how to relax, whether I was sitting on an aeroplane, at a dinner party or in a meeting, and brought a whole new dimension to my life. It took quite a long time to get used to it, but in particular I used to put it into practice when I came home in the evenings after being on the go the whole time. I would lie down for fifteen or twenty minutes and get into the 'sleep', waking up later completely refreshed.

When you are able to feel this total relaxation coming over you, you really feel you are going to die. It is the most amazing sensation. You are then in a sort of limbo state – even though you are awake. The Maharishi told me, 'When you are tired, you should never go to sleep -- you should only sleep at night. But you will now 'sleep' whilst wide awake, and if somebody startles you in the middle of it you will come to in a startled state.' It was thus essential to try and maintain the fifteen or twenty minutes without interruption, and I could feel the energy going through me, replaced by a wonderful feeling of all the tension going out of the body. My lifestyle now is not so hectic and so I do not have the need to practice this often, but I still do it from time to time. It was worth all the trips to India just to have had the opportunity of meeting that wonderful, great man. I tried to get him to come over on a trip to this part of the world, but he was so involved with kings and dignitaries that he didn't have any time to spare.

With this new 'jewel in my box', so to speak, coupled with the fact that I had and still have very low blood pressure, I was able to stand up to the trials of everyday life which you can see around you all the time. Drivers in their cars in a 'white knuckle' state, everybody in a rush. If everyone in the world could have access to a man like the Maharishi life would take on a new dimension, but unfortunately not everyone has such an opportunity as I did.

I also had the pleasure of playing some golf in India, which was quite an experience. I say this because for a start we each had four caddies: one to carry the clubs, one to put the ball down, one to go ahead with pieces of cloth to cover the balls so they didn't get nicked by the large raven-like birds, and the fourth to clean the clubs after they were used. There were four of us with four caddies apiece, so twenty of us in all went the round; quite a remarkable experience when you're not used to that sort of treatment.

To have one caddy in this day and age is rare, because they are few and far between, so the whole thing was marvellous. We had breakfast at the halfway house, having started off at something like five o'clock in the morning before it became too hot to play. Yet another wonderful memory of India.

When I went to stay with friends of mine in Bombay in their town residence the building contained two hundred and fifty servants amongst the four floors housing them and other members of their family. No matter where you went, when you came to a door a hand opened it. During one reception they gave for me another guest dropped his glass on the floor. He didn't look right, left or down, and in a flash one of the servants came and cleared it up in seconds, while the guest just carried on talking as if nothing had happened. I had a car placed at my disposal and the driver was there twenty-four hours a day. He wasn't allowed to sleep in the car so he slept in the bushes, and when I stepped up to the car he was there. All this was just a remarkable example of the two opposites of wealth and poverty. The former was shown to extremes by an Indian prince I met at a reception, who was in love with a young lady who lived a couple of hundred miles away. He owned a DC3 aircraft, which he sent down to her every day completely full of roses.

One of my most wonderful trips was flying along the tips of the Himalayan mountains in a small light aircraft – an experience beyond belief. It was not the first time I had been in a small aircraft. The first time was in 1955 when I went to an air show in Toronto, and always being game for anything I went up in a Tiger Moth aircraft owned by two Chinese chaps called the Wong brothers. The lady pilot took me up to a fair old height, and then informed me that I was her first commercial passenger and would I mind if she did a couple of loop-the-loops! This she did, and needless to say that was yet another experience I shall never forget.

The place, above all that has always called me back – and I've been there over fifty times – is South Africa. It was a fascinating place when I first went there and I had many adventures, as I shall later relate.

Norris McWhirter, publisher of the *Guinness Book of Records,* presenting a copy of the book to Tommie Campbell, 1969.

Tommie Campbell world record holder for the longest golf drive of 392 yards.

The author *(centre)* with Rex Fleet *(left)*, Managing Director of NCR Limited and Michael Alderson, Managing Director of Golf World Limited, after signing the agreement for NCR to sponsor the 1979 Long Drive Golf Championship.

All Stars, Woburn, 1985. Tommie Campbell chipping to the eighteenth hole.

EVENING PRESS

TUESDAY, DECEMBER 1, 1981

Vol. 27; (48th Week) (No. 285) Price 15p

£1m fire hits 'freedom in sport' golfer

6th

Gardaí are investigating a £1 million blaze at a warehouse owned by a sportsman who was founder and chairman of the "Freedom in Sport" organisation, which upholds the right of players to visit South Africa.

The alert was raised at 10 o'clock last night when flames were seen shooting through the roof by security guard Peter Smith, who patrolled the premises and the adjoining cul-de-sacs.

Mr. Smith said today: "I spotted the fire at the gable end and I rushed to the 'phone, but within five minutes the flames had engulfed half the factory. The fire brigade had no chance to save it."

Mr. Graham Campbell, the...

After the fire, forensic experts found a clear link between the Campbells managing director's firm at the Sevenoaks-based T.C. Canvas, and the adjoining Woolfson premises at Greenhills Rd., Walkinstown. £10,000 worth of damage was caused by the evening's blaze, but police have made no arrests as to who is responsible.

The warehouse was housing over 300 rolls of carpet. It belongs to the T.C. Canvas Council which were destroyed by the fire. Damage was also caused to the second fire outside the premises owned by Weatherglaze Window Co.

Mr. Tommy Campbell was founder and chairman of the Freedom in Sport organisation, the aims of which are to uphold the right of the individual to true freedom of choice in every sphere 'especially sporting interests.'

Mr. Campbell was also a member of the South African Sport Council (SASCOC) and has been accused by the organisation in "promoting apartheid sport."

A keen golfer, he is now listed in the Guinness Book of Records for the longest golfing drive on record—a distance of 392 yards—which he achieved in July, 1964, at Patrick Golf Club.

He fell foul of the South...

One of the front page headlines from when Tommie Campbell's business was burned down.

Tommie Campbell with his old friend Matt Busby, former manager of Manchester United FC, and Brian Hugget MBE, former Ryder Cup player.

The author with Ken Wolstenholme.

Chapter Eight
The World Famous Golf Drive

'What's all this about a long golf drive – are you the fellow in the *Guinness Book of Records* – I suppose it was a fluke – does it happen often?' Time after time these and many other questions arise and you never get away from it, which I suppose is understandable. I could always identify an air of disbelief in their curiosity, as if they were trying to catch me out or discover some angle which no one had thought about before. I can safely say I have heard them all, but then I suppose in many cases when I appear before them or am introduced to them they are immediately surprised to see a chap only five feet eight inches tall and weighing round eleven stone.

Norris McWhirter, the original publisher of the *Guinness Book of Records*, said to me one day, 'Something will be written about you somewhere in the world every day.' He said this was because mine was the type of record which attracts attention, and apart from the ordinary general public there are millions of golfers out there, many of whom would pay money just to get another ten or twenty yards onto their drives.

Was it a fluke? No it wasn't. It happened at a golf course outside Dun Laoghaire which to those not conversant with the Gaelic language means 'King's Town'. In fact, in the early years when the name was changed the notepaper of the club used to read 'Dun Laoghaire' with King's Town in brackets afterwards. However, this was offensive to some of the members and eventually the King's Town was dropped.

On that particular day there was a competition which include a feature, 'longest drive from the tee on the eighteenth hole'. It was then, and I'm sure it still is, a par five. Did I have any special equipment? No I did not. The actual driver I used was indeed a ladies', a Jean Donald with one change. I had a stiff men's shaft inserted into the head and it weighed twelve ounces, which I have quoted many times to disprove the theory that you must have a heavy driver to hit the ball a long way. You don't use a baseball bat to swat a fly!

Unfortunately, that particular club was stolen and despite the efforts of my friends and the media's offering a reward, it never turned up. Maybe the person who took it will read this book and hopefully get in touch with me because I would like to have it back. The ball was a standard Dunlop 65, number 3. There was, I should mention at this stage, drama attached to this also, because the makers wished to have it mounted in black Kilkenny marble, and then to my horror Dunlop lost it. I also had an offer of ten thousand dollars for that particular ball from a gentleman called Mr Phillips in Long Island, New York, and I remember at one particular event approaching an official of the R&A enquiring if they would have any objection to my taking that money. I got very short shrift and was told that if I took it it would place my amateur status in jeopardy, so that was the end of that. The fact that the ball had been lost got to the media – if it hadn't I would have asked Dunlop to substitute another in its place, no one would have known any different – a golf ball is a golf ball.

Coming to the actual day again, it was overcast; it had been raining and there was still a slight drizzle and no wind whatsoever; it was also very calm. These last two factors are important because it meant there was practically no run on the ball and no wind to assist me. My partner on that day was a dear old friend called Harry Gaw and carrying my clubs was a caddy from my home course, Foxrock Golf Club, one of life's great characters called Tom Clack who lived nearby in Dun Laoghaire and used to walk to and from Foxrock every day of his life. He was with me in many of my triumphs, always urging me on in his rich Dublin accent. Each utterance was punctuated by the Holy Name, which he pronounced 'Jasus'.

He had some remarkable sayings which just came out naturally, and I remember one time when he was caddying for me and he didn't look at all well. I knew that he had been ill and confined to bed, which was very unusual for him. It was a Saturday morning and I enquired, 'Clack, I haven't seen you for some time, and I understand you were sick. How are you feeling now?'

'Oh, a lot better thanks. As a matter of fact the doctor came to see me yesterday and said if I feel up to it I can get up on Monday.' It put me in mind of another great 'Irishism' which came from a porter in Dublin Airport, and which I have mentioned many times and other people have used it – as I came out I was greeted by this chap, 'Hello, give me those bags Mr Campbell, and follow me, I'm right behind you.' These great characters have now departed this life, and I wonder if Clack is caddying for Harry in Heaven.

Well, back to the drive again – the terms of reference were straightforward enough. The ball had to land within a specified area of the fairway, which was approximately forty yards wide. The other stipulation was to hit it as hard as you could! I then turned to Clack and said, 'We'd better take a new ball here, Clack – hopefully it will go further.' With that he opened the bag and took out a new Dunlop 65, which was nicely wrapped in coloured paper, as they were in those days. I always remember the number on it was 3.

Well, I hit it and knew from the moment of contact that it was a big one; you get that feeling coming up from the head of the club through the shaft into your hands. It's a wonderful sensation that only you can appreciate and is one of the things that makes golf such a fascinating game. However, the ball soared off the club face – I used to always get a great flight on my 'good drives' and because I hit it so hard, the club head was travelling in the region of 140 mph, I bent the ball like an aspirin, which meant that after a period in the air when other drives would begin to descend, mine took on a double flight and started to rise again. The guy who was responsible for marking out the drives that day said it went over his head with a 'swish' like a rocket.

Fortunately it came to rest in the middle of the fairway, which was okay, watched in amazement by a group of people, one of whom was a well-known reporter named Joe Sherwood who was to play a major role in this whole affair, and was indeed the self-starter to all that followed. His first reacting was to instruct the official not to move the marker because he said he wanted that particular drive of mine measured, as it could be a world record. By this time I had departed into the club house never for a moment thinking or imagining what was about to happen.

Sure enough, Joe made sure the resting place of my ball was properly recorded, in fact he had a special mark made on a small tree in line with the actual finishing point of my drive. He then went further and had it measured very carefully with a link chain. If he had not been around it would probably all have been forgotten, but having satisfied himself on all counts he published his findings in the national newspaper for which he worked, and this was the first time those magic numbers appeared in print – 392. That was the yardage from start to finish that went into the record books.

It was also important that he was there because in later years there were those who said that nobody could hit a ball that distance, and indeed suggested that it was not my ball and was one that came from the sixteenth tee, which was a hole running alongside the eighteenth fairway. The Irish are not particularly good at bestowing compliments on their own and have not been called a nation of 'knockers' for nothing.

There have been so many things written about it in so many magazines, books and newspapers all over the world, but one particular person I think confirmed what I just said when he called me up one day and asked if I would play a few holes of golf with him at his home club, which was The Castle in County Dublin. His name was Ulick O'Connor, who at that time was writing a series of essays for the London *Times* on famous people. Ulick is a very well-known author having written Brendan Behan's biography and another one on Oliver St John Gogarty. I would like to quote some of the things he said in the article he wrote about me – entitled, 'The Loneliness of the Long Distance Driver' – following the few holes of golf which we played that day. I should add at this time he was a keen golfer himself.

> We walked out onto the fourteenth tee at Castle Golf Club last week, and I decided we would only play the long holes to give room for Tommie's drives. He teed the ball high and hit it 315 yards down the fairway. What was curious was it didn't look a different swing from any other except that there was more of a 'swish' sound at the end. I thought I'd watch more carefully on the next drive as we moved to the 504 yards sixteenth. This time I noticed he didn't let the club head touch the ground before addressing the ball. He went back as far as possible on the wind-up. He is extremely supple at the waist so he can get his left shoulder up without any strain.

Then the club came down with the same swishing sound and the ball landed 325 yards away. We then came to the seventeenth, and Tommie was explaining to me how he could keep his left heel on the ground which gave him the effect of being coiled up like a spring, and on this occasion I watched very closely. There wasn't the slightest indication of force, only a smooth rhythmic movement like the pendulum of a grandfather clock. This time the ball took off as if it had a secondary rocket to project it and landed 350 yards away. It is worth noting that Tommie at this time was fifty-one years of age, and each of those drives were measured by me. There wasn't any wind, or any assistance, and it was one of the most remarkable occasions in my sporting career.

Coming back to my statement that the Irish are a nation of knockers, I would again quote from Ulick's articles as follows:

> I thought of the taxi driver the night before who, when I told him I was going to play with Tommie Campbell, said, For Jesus sake, that drive bounced off a stone!

Ulick continues,

> Well, that's Dublin for you, the only city in the world that has produced three Nobel prizes for literature and where every yobbo can do better, and where they tell you now that their only record holder in golf bounced the ball off a stone to make his record-breaking drive.

The article was dated 9th August, 1981.

I might add at this juncture that I have received very few compliments, and it's something that you must learn to live with and not become agitated in any way. It's rather like being the fastest gun in the West – everybody wants to have a go at you. Over the years I have received many letters too numerous to mention, a good number of which have contained challenges of one sort or another. Things like, 'We have a fellow in our club who can hit the ball further that you can', 'I don't believe it' – and others quite nasty and meant to be so. I suppose that is the price of fame, and it has never affected me too much and it's as active today as ever but I've learned to go with it.

However, the next big moment came when the news of my feat reached the ears of the *Guinness Book of Records*, which was published by a company called Guinness Superlatives Limited. They were excited about this drive and set in motion their investigation, which consisted of proper written confirmations, together with a check on Joe's yardage, which proved to be correct. It took eighteen months to ratify, and then in 1966 – the drive having taken place in 1964 – my entry appeared in the great book. It was also the beginning of a long-standing friendship with the publisher, Norris McWhirter, who is a remarkable man with an incredible memory for all kinds of facts and figures.

Once this happens, look out. The power of the *Guinness Book of Records* is awesome and, in short, your life is never the same again. Millions read it and refer to it for all sorts of records, it is the world's number one Christmas present and is printed in many different languages. It is a funny feeling when the realisation hits you that out of all the tens of millions of golfers hitting balls every day all over the world, you have achieved something that no one else has done.

Of course people have hit golf balls further in all sorts of freak conditions – on frozen lakes and airport runways –

indeed I have hit the ball further on a number of occasions. One happened when I was sixty-two years of age and playing the thirteenth hole at the Royal Cinque Ports Golf Club in Deal, Kent. I drove the ball from that tee a distance which was measured by a club official as 419 yards, and it is worth recording because of my age at that time, which was probably another record. After it appeared in the national press a number of outside well-wishers, including one top international golf publication suggested to the club it would be rather a nice idea to have a plaque commemorating this feat on the tee from where the ball was hit. Indeed, they offered to pay the cost involved but the committee in their wisdom felt this was not really anything special and therefore took no action. I think this was a pity because people like to read about famous shots on golf courses and it was something which no one had ever done before and may never do again.

One amusing incident about that particular drive concerned the two gentlemen who were playing in front of me. They were putting out on the green when suddenly this ball arrived. Those who are familiar with the hole will know it's not possible to see the actual tee from the green because of the contours of the ground, so they were mystified as to where the ball had come from. One of them said he had contemplated putting it in his pocket! The mystery was solved when they waited on the nearby fourteenth tee to see what would happen, and when I arrived at the ball they kindly enquired about the circumstances and were very complimentary on discovering it was my drive. The incident has now become history and I am sure it will be talked about for many days to come.

One thing it did for me, and there were other occasions as well, was to remove the 'fluke' element so many good people kept continually referring to, I also won a long driving competition in 1970 against some of the top professionals in the game, and many other events over the years. I know this probably sounds very boastful but I would not like people to think my record was one of those freak things – mind you I have been called a freak on many occasions. Norris McWhirter said it was something I was born with and, I might add in answer to many questions, it did not happen all the time. Yes, I always hit the ball a long way but on the occasions when this thing happens the ball just goes twenty or thirty yards further. It can be a nuisance and indeed has cost me dearly in competitions when I have maybe a shot of 120 yards and get what they call a 'flyer' and the ball ends up sailing over the green!

I remember one competition at the well-known golf club of Moor Allerton in Yorkshire when I was playing a hole – the eighteenth I think as there were people in the background having tea – and I hit this 7 iron when the 'gear change' happened inside me and the ball went flying over the green and scattered a whole bunch of people who were waiting to remonstrate with me when I arrived up at the green.

The record remained in the *Guinness Book of Records* for twenty-six years and then it was taken out. The reason this decision was made arose from a series of events taking place all over the world, and the publishers quite rightly said that it couldn't go on any longer and it would have to be changed. What in fact was happening was that people were getting special drivers made with longer shafts and all sorts of things just for the purpose of hitting the ball to create a record. These 'achievements' were coming in from places like Johannesburg, where they are thousands of feet up so the ball goes further – and all sorts of funny places and circumstances, so that the whole thing was really becoming farcical. In the end Guinness came to the conclusion that there would have to be a new record put into the book and the condition would be the person must use regular equipment that can be bought in any shop, and the ball must be a standard ball bought in the same circumstances. The record would be how far the ball carried through the air and not how far it went after hitting the ground.

That is the status quo at the time. Certainly these boys today with their modern equipment hit the ball a very long way, and I've often been asked the question, how far would I have hit it in 1964 if I had had the equipment and the balls which are available today. I guess we will never know!

Chapter Nine
South Africa

It was in 1968 that I received an invitation to play in the South African Dunlop Masters, which I accepted, and this heralded the beginning of a long association with that wonderful country.

I duly made my way down there, not really knowing a good deal about it, and remember arriving at Jan Smuts airport in Johannesburg, which was all very new to me. Whilst I was waiting in the customs clearance hall for my luggage and golf clubs, I saw a pile of local newspapers, and to my amazement (and trepidation) noticed a picture on the front page with the heading 'Look out for this man'. There under the heading was a picture of yours truly. This brought me down to earth with a jolt, because they had written up all the usual stuff about long driving, *Guinness Book of Records* and so on. Here was I, an amateur, coming to play with all the professionals, so the last thing in the world I wanted was this sort of advance publicity. However, there was nothing I could do about it so I decided to act the part and do the best I could.

After my luggage had been cleared the next thing was to hail a taxi, which set off at high speed from the airport. I mention this because of an incident that happened about halfway from the airport into the outskirts of Johannesburg, and it involved a young black youth who was crossing the road at a rather slow pace, though he must have seen the taxi coming. This galvanised the driver into immediate action, which I could hardly believe, whereby he put his foot hard on the accelerator and drove straight at the young chap. This spurred the lad into action himself, and he took off like a gazelle onto the pathway, at which the taxi driver yelled, 'Goddam it! I've missed the little bugger!'

It suddenly began to dawn on me that he had really meant to knock the lad off the road, and I thought to myself, *Hello, what's all this?* I didn't make any comment about it but it was one of the first impressions I had of the great problem which was there and which, to be perfectly honest, I didn't really understand. It was a self-starter to many visits over the next twenty years to that part of the world, and it gave me a real insight into some of the basic problems and fears which were very prevalent at the time.

The actual golf part of the trip wasn't very important – there was the usual leg-pulling, which I had become accustomed to at the time, and finally I found myself on the first day, on the first tee, in front of thousands of people playing with a world famous golfer, and listening to the sales sports manager of Dunlop at the time announcing me onto the tee. It went something like this, 'And now ladies and gentlemen, it gives me very great pleasure to welcome from Ireland Tommie Campbell, who as you know appears in the *Guinness Book of World Records* for the longest drive in competitive golf – a distance of three hundred and ninety-two yards.'

Then he went on to list various other achievements which had happened to me, and when he went on to mention again the three hundred and ninety-two yards I could see all the people looking at the card to see the distance of the first hole. As far as I can recall it was three hundred and forty-two yards and no doubt they were wondering whether I would use my driver or some lesser instrument; the sense of anticipation was great indeed. There is an incredible silence which follows the final statement to the people at large, 'Quiet please ladies and gentlemen', and then there you are on your own in front of thousands of people. It wasn't a particularly nice day, there was a gentle breeze blowing up into my face, and there I was wishing I had never had anything to do with world records, or long drives, and wondering what I was going to do, whether I would miss it, whether I would hit someone down the side. All that being the feeling on only the first hole, with seventeen more to go that first day, and three more days play to follow. I mention all this because it shows the other side to the glamour which people think of as being associated with a famous person. However, I need not have worried because I played quite well and made a lot of friends.

At that particular juncture I learned some things about South Africa, apart from the fact that it is a very beautiful country. As I went in the capacity of a visitor along the main motorways and suggested routes, I found they had bypassed the townships, so one could take a holiday in South Africa in all the beautiful places and never see a black township. This of course had been deliberately planned.

Being down there and being in a business which was international, I tried to examine the possibilities of some collaboration in my particular market, but found it extremely difficult. I never really knew where I was and the general standards of ethics and moral responsibility were very different to what I had been used to. I therefore decided it was not really a commercial prospect for us. One of the interesting moments on that trip was going into a certain bar in Durban which had a rule that there were 'no rounds', in other words you could not buy a round, so if you were with four or five people each person got a tab and everyone ordered as they felt like it. I thought that this was a very sensible system, because it meant that if anyone wanted to drink quicker than everyone else no one felt they had to keep up with him or her, and could happily drink at their own level. I have never come across that anywhere else in the world.

I had moved from Johannesburg down to Durban to participate in some things there. I remember walking from my hotel to the sea front and being confronted by a small black boy, who asked me if I could fetch him a bucket of water from the sea, at which I realised that he was not allowed to go and get it himself because that part of the beach – indeed most of the beach – was for whites only. That was a situation which could not be contravened, and indeed I saw policemen on a regular basis evicting people who had been sleeping there rough at night, which was very disconcerting.

Durban was not only beautiful – it was also very complex. There was a large population of Indian extraction living there who were not popular with the black population, and vice versa, and in earlier years there had been some very serious confrontations. Being interested, I enquired about the matter, and discovered that the Indians had been imported to harvest the sugar plantations in Natal and no one had bothered about what might happen to them after they were no longer required. They were just left to fend for themselves. This they seemed to be doing quite well in terms of the achievements attained by their children in the schools and their general position in the community, but it was not a very healthy state of affairs.

I had made up my mind that one of the greatest mistakes ever made by a country was the introduction by South Africa of *apartheid*. It cost them untold billions with all the added side effects about which we all know.

The situation of course deteriorated and I found myself becoming involved years later in 1981 when things were beginning to hot up. Nelson Mandela was in jail, there were protests in many parts of the world, and one of the effects as far as sport was concerned was that there seemed to be a 50–50 chance of South Africa 'wrecking' some of our sports as we knew them in their traditional and familiar form.

I found myself involved with a number of other sports people, and we decided to look into this whole question of political interference in sport. We saw that the main problem area was South Africa. I made many visits to observe and see what the actual situation was, and learned many things – including some very important aspects such as the fact that you could only look at South Africa in an African dimension that it was suffering from a lot of long-range meddlers who did not really understand the problem, and that there were freeloaders cashing in on the whole situation.

I met all kinds of people – top politicians, top sportsmen and women from the South African end and it didn't take long to eliminate the problem which we had all seen in other areas before. One problem which came back into my mind was from the middle fifties, when we had business involvements in Cyprus it was obvious from speaking to the two communities that there was going to be trouble between the Greek and Turkish populations and that it would be soon. I remember voicing this opinion in the English-speaking club at Nicosia and the only way I can describe the reaction was that I might as well have been talking to the wall. Nobody took the slightest interest, and we all know what happened in Cyprus as a result, and it is still living with us today.

I could see the same thing in South Africa, and my judgement of the situation was basic in that most of those in authority within the white community realised that their time was running out, and that they could not carry on the way they had in the past and that something had to be done by making the best deal possible. This was never a runner, as they found out, and indeed as I found out, because the decisions of the black community were not made in South Africa – they were made by people in distant lands who for whatever reason had had to get out. There was therefore no point in going to South Africa to meet non-white leaders because it was an exercise in futility. I found it interesting because I visited many coloured and black communities and looked at their sports facilities, which were all in a state of abject despair. I would ask them why they didn't get rid of the weeds, and try and make the places look nice, and the answer was always the same, 'That is not our job, we have been instructed not to do it,' thus creating a terrible impasse.

The bottom line was that there was no way they would do anything if they had been instructed not to – they were terrified of the consequences should they, for example, move into one of the state houses which were being offered. I saw one family who did that, they were set upon and their furniture burned. Of course there were all the do-gooders who came and said this and that. One particular lady who wanted to see me called on me on what was a beautiful day.

I made some remark to that effect, to which she replied that it may be a beautiful day for some but not for the black community in South Africa. She went on to say that though she was white her heart was black, and continued a long diatribe on the theme of what her thoughts were. I asked her what she was going to do, and pointed out that she was probably doing more harm than good and that the basic non-white community were not interested in her. Investigation showed that she had wanted to go into a particular event in one of the non-white communities and the police had warned her that it would be dangerous to go in. She ignored the warning and soon her blue Volkswagen was hurtling into the area. On entry it was met by a fusillade of bottles and stones and the authorities had a job to get her out alive.

Those are the realities of such a situation. I remember another incident in Cape Town when Senator Ted Kennedy came along to see what he could make out of it all. I happened to be there when he arrived for a meeting at Government House, when there were a lot of press men around. He stood up and said, 'Gentlemen, last night I had one of the greatest nights of my life – I spent it in black Soweto.'

He then stood back with his chest stuck out, while there was a perceptive silence, broken by a little New York reporter who said, 'Senator, may I ask have you ever spent a night in Black Harlem in New York?' That took the wind out of the senator's sails and exposed what he was up to, which was the end of that particular press conference. These people who kept appearing down there and hopping on the bandwagon really were not doing any good.

I went to many schools and spoke to the students, because South Africa was a very sports-conscious country. I asked boys who were coming to an age when they could play for their country if they were disappointed that they might never play in a great stadium elsewhere in the world like Murrayfield, New Zealand, Twickenham, and was met with a stony silence. I could not get any enthusiasm whatsoever. They all seemed to be absolutely indoctrinated that that was the way it was going to be and I'm afraid that on that particular point any dialogue or discussion came up against a brick wall.

The sports administrators generally did not have a clue as to how things should be handled. They were far too old and had been in office far too long, but in that particular area I met one of the most interesting men and became great friends with him. He was the head of the South African Rugby Board, Danie Craven. I believe I was the only outside member to be privileged to attend an inner sanctum meeting of the South African Rugby Board, which was very interesting. It was obvious what it had been before and dear old Danie had once been quoted as saying that no black person would put on a Springboks rugby blazer except over his dead body, but time is a great healer and he had changed. He worked very hard to get the international community to see his point of view, but as I told him, the situation was political and there was no logic or common sense to it. By all means he should keep on with what he was doing but he was wasting his time. His answer was to revert to rebel tours which brought another breed of people into South Africa promising this, that and the other thing, and as history shows there were some rebel tours including one by South Africa to New Zealand which turned out to be a terrible disaster. I told Danie there was no future in such tours until the political situation was resolved, but that he should try and prepare the ground for the crop that would eventually be sown and hope that it would reap a reasonable harvest in the future.

He was coming round to this way of thinking but there were still a number of die-hards who could not see further than their noses and were up to all sorts of antics which were putting things back and not moving them forward at all. In the end Danie came to me and asked what he should do. After deliberations we agreed that there should be a congress, which was eventually held in 1983 in South Africa. I assisted with this congress which ended up with eighty-six media and sports people coming in from all over the world. It turned out to be a great success and the fact they allowed people to go where they wanted to go was a real eye-opener to those who came along – even the most ardent anti-South Africans. At the same time it was only an exercise in public relations and was never going to give any stability to South Africa or the situation there.

I had many discussions with politicians and people like Danie Craven outside of South Africa also, during which I voiced the opinion that there was only one solution. Because of the complex makeup of South Africa, which in many cases was tribal with two major groups – the Zulus and the Xhosas – these people had never in history been able to live together, and many of them had no idea about government or what was going on. There were about eighteen million of them, and four million whites and that gave rise to a very complex situation.

Something like fifty visits to the country and many, many interviews and talks brought me to the conclusion that there was only one person who could possibly unite all these factions into some sort of mass and bring a temporary peace to South Africa. That man was Nelson Mandela. There was nobody else within light years of him and I made it my business to find out quite a bit about the situation concerning him. As we all know now he had a rough time but the outcome was inevitable; I knew it was going to happen, and I tried to build on this fact with the sports people and start things moving, but it was just impossible.

During 1983 I recall having breakfast in Johannesburg and sat nearby was Bishop Desmond Tutu with another well-known church dignitary. I approached him to know if he would like to be involved in the congress we were having, and he simply did not want to know. He had already declared, in his arm-waving style, that children were not to go to school and so on, and when I asked him if he would be prepared to accept the responsibility for millions of illiterate teenagers in South Africa he became quite agitated and angry. This showed to me that at that stage he was not prepared to get down to basic dialogue with the different parties – it was all publicity orientated though perhaps he did mean well. However, I was not at all impressed and this memory has stayed with me since that day.

It came about that in 1986 I decided I could do nothing more in South Africa, though it seemed to always call me back. I had been knocked back by so many people for trying to help and advise in my own way, and I was very disillusioned and unhappy about a number of aspects of this wonderful country with such great potential.

All the rebel tours came and went, the freeloaders came and went, the right-wingers said one thing and the left said another. Then came that great day when Nelson Mandela was released and took over the reins. I think that what he has done will go down as one of the greatest diplomatic achievements in world history. My fervent hope is that when he decides to step down from the high office he now holds there will be somebody able to carry on his great work and manage what he has achieved – but only time will tell.

A more sinister element crept into my South African experiences when it became common knowledge that I had been trying to do something, and this was followed by threats on my life and many other strange happenings, the culmination of which was the burning down of my businesses. Whilst there was no proof I have no doubt in my mind it came about as a result of my involvement with South Africa. When things like this happen there are always side effects. One was the attitude of our insurance company who did not want to pay up, and I would like to use this opportunity to advise everyone to check their insurance. Most people who sell insurance are sharks and there are so many pitfalls in the small print which the average person does not understand or even read.

It is nice to see that since all those problems over ten years ago things have brightened in South Africa. Their rugby team has won the world cup, their golfers and athletes have been able to participate under the South African flag and bring great credit and pride to their country. I hope that this will continue and that South Africa can become the dominating influence in Africa which it should have been many, many years ago. They have a lot to give, but when Nelson Mandela took over, there was no African model to copy. All of the countries who had gained their independence had been wracked with corruption, as we read in the newspapers almost every week. Despite all this South Africa holds great affection for me and I wish that beautiful country well.

Chapter Ten
So What!

Being in the *Guinness Book of Records* I've been here and there and met many famous and infamous people. I believe you have to ask yourself the question, 'Does anybody really give a damn? Are you looking for pats on the back? Is your family proud of you? Do people think you are a pain in the neck? Are you staying the course?'

Other pertinent questions are, 'What have you really achieved and where are you now? What have you learned and what will you do in the future?' I have always tried to keep a level head in all things, and though being in the *Guinness Book of Records* is not something they can take away from you, it is not always a bed of roses. You could say it has side effects, and some of those would very quickly bring you back to earth if that is what you need.

In terms of attitude there are two kinds of people. First of all there are those with whom you are associated through sport whom you know either well or vaguely, and I can safely say that it is very very seldom that any of those ever come and say something pleasant or sincere. In virtually every case it is some sort of sarcastic or snide remark like, 'the ball must have hit a stone', or 'it was a fluke'. If anyone can come up with a new remark not heard before I would be amazed. What causes people to be like this? Maybe it is the green horns of jealousy, but you have to learn to take it all with a smile on your face and not retaliate, but shrug your shoulders and walk away.

On the other side of the coin are the general public, who don't know you on a personal basis but who are aware of who you are. There have been a number of pleasant moments with people I have never seen or heard about before, who have come up and said nice things. I remember having breakfast one time in South Africa and a man left his family at another table and brought me across a book which was signed 'from an ordinary South African family to someone who has given us great pleasure – we are proud to have met you'.

There is an old saying, 'never meet your heroes' and I can certainly vouch for that because having met many great names on a one-to-one basis I was unimpressed in the majority of cases. When you look at their backgrounds and where some of them came from it is not really surprising. I have always said I hope I do not fall into that category, and hope I have carried the honour with dignity and not talked about it too much. Believe it or not I have never liked talking about myself, so people will ask, 'Why then is he writing this book?' At the moment I don't have an answer to that.

Studying people has always been and still is a hobby of mine and as far as I can remember I started doing this when I first went on the road to sell at the early age of nineteen, going on twenty. With no previous experience in that field I had to find things out for myself, and quickly discovered that as far as the people I was trying to sell to were concerned they were in three main categories – the good, the bad and the ugly! This meant I had to develop a different psychology for each of them. I will always remember my first sale, made in June 1947, when I was just one month away from my twentieth birthday. The product I was selling was raw wool and the customer was a well known woollen manufacturer in a lovely little village in the west of

Ireland called Foxford, in County Mayo. These people made beautiful Foxford blankets and tweeds from one hundred per cent wool, indeed I believe there are still some of these in use within our family today.

One unusual feature about that particular establishment was that it was owned by an order of nuns, and I remember in my silly way wondering whether I would be shown the door if they found out I was a Protestant, which unfortunately was the way one was brought up to think in those particular times. The manager was a Mr Seamus Sherry, who was a very pleasant and efficient gentleman, and who turned out to be a good friend of mine for the rest of his life. He ran the establishment superbly – every corner of it was spotlessly clean. I know this because he took me on a tour of the building which was most interesting, and I also remember one particular stage of the tour when the bells of the convent next door sounded twelve o'clock. This signalled a custom that when that time of day – known as the Angelus – came around everyone stopped, crossed themselves and said a prayer.

In my own clumsy way I decided to do the same thing but when we were back in the office Seamus said to me that I had carried out the ritual of crossing myself the wrong way round. He said, 'Tommie, I realise that you are not one of us but you are still a child of God and very welcome in this establishment.' He offered me tea while we talked about my wool samples. The beverage duly arrived served in beautiful china cups, and with some lovely home-made biscuits. Over this we cemented a friendship which lasted a very long time, and I will always cherish it, because on that day I learned a lot about people, and my faith in human nature received a boost.

I walked out of there on air and could not get to a phone quick enough to report the good news to my boss, Charlie, who received it with great enthusiasm and encouragement.

Driving away I could not help calculating in my mind how much commission I had made, and as I recall it came to what was then a very large sum of money – sixty-three pounds. I was on my way, and never looked back from that sale, going from strength to strength from then on.

I should say that prior to that occasion I had received an excellent education from my boss which I didn't really appreciate until later. He was a great disciplinarian who made sure that a suit was always worn, with a clean shirt and shoes neatly polished, all topped off with what was called a soft hat. Punctuality was paramount, and I can say that there was never any time in my life when I was late for any occasion or appointment. I am sure that in later years I have driven my family mad by always wanting to leave plenty of time in hand, but that's the way I was brought up. The boss always insisted that we called the customers 'sir' and greeted them with 'Good morning', also that we never smoked unless one was offered. In those days everybody seemed to smoke, it was the self-starter to many meetings and seemed to break down any barriers that might have existed.

The other piece of sound advice that Charlie gave me was, 'When you have had your say, shut up! Don't go on with unnecessary chatter, get out of the office diplomatically and quietly, just in case the buyer might change his mind.'

I met all sorts of buyers all over the world and sometimes they were the owners of the various companies. It was always a position of great importance in those days because the basic raw material was the most important thing they bought and there was a lot of competition.

One particular buyer I shall never forget, and who turned out to be a good friend later, always greeted you in his office accompanied by a large dog and he had a knack which I have never seen anywhere else. When he was presented with a sample of wool he would take a staple from it and with a quick flick of his finger would snap it in half. This was very demoralising because, one of the important things with all grades of wool was its tensile strength, and to see for the first time a man doing this before your eyes could knock your confidence right out of the window. After he had done it there was the usual patter of, 'Well, that's not very good,' but what he was doing of course was breaking you down to try to buy your product cheaper.

Coming back to my first meeting with this gentleman, and after he had performed the 'knack' he turned round to me and said, 'Well, that wool is not very good, is it?'

I remember smiling at him and saying, 'I wonder if you could teach me that trick, sir?' He broke into a smile, realising I had rumbled him, and became a very good customer of ours for many years to come. I suppose in a way we are all sales people at heart – some are better at it that others, because it is an art and if you analyse the good and great sales people you will find that they sell everything they have and in most cases don't really realise they are doing so. What I mean by that is that they will 'sell' their house ('It's a lovely house, beautiful garden') they 'sell' the car they drive, their holidays, their golf clubs and so on. It's just born in them and if they can ally that to trust and the ability to deliver, then they are real diamonds.

I could only sell something in which I had full confidence, and if it was everything which I said it was, because I always liked to feel that I could go back to that person any time and not fall into the category of what I call 'sell and bunk'. There are too many of these people selling wrong pensions, dodgy investments and so on. So much of this goes on today, and the only advice I can give to people is to make absolutely sure to read the small print. If you are selling something to the public, bearing in mind that last remark of mine, one thing you must remember is that it takes a long time before your product – should it be a new one – is noticed, and many people wrongly decide to change their advertising and promotion just at a time when people are beginning to notice it.

In all these instances, as far as the general public are concerned, I have always said to myself if a little old lady of eighty with white hair and wearing tennis shoes understands it, then do it! I have found that people generally don't vary very much, and they all tend to move like sheep together. They are not very adventurous and tend to stick to a pattern that may well have been in their family for a long time. For example, I have met people who buy most of their clothes and items through mail order because their mothers did it, or who go to such-and-such a shop because their parents went there, stay with the same butcher, etc. – all pointers to be borne in mind.

The public can also be very fickle – you are judged on your last performance – and in sporting parlance you can run onto a pitch in an international match as a great hero, and leave it as a bum. That's the way it is, and it's not going to change, so you have to learn to cope with it, learn to focus, learn to stay the course and don't go into the wilderness because people forget about you very easily. Indeed, the expression that I have heard more than any other with regard to sport is, 'Whatever happened to so-and-so?'

As I have been writing this a terrible tragedy has hit the world, and that is the death of Princess Diana, and its effect on people of all denominations and all classes throughout the globe. My fervent hope is that this great coming together of people will bring about more consideration for others, that people will stop and think about things they have done before which are not kind to their fellow man. Princess Diana turned the whole world on its head – let her efforts not be in vain.

Chapter Eleven
Never Meet Your Heroes

I remember saying this to a lady in the course of conversation one time and will always remember her answer, which was, 'I never see my hero – he's always at the bloody golf club!' which reminds me of a little ditty which goes like this.

The Golfer

> 'Who's that stranger, mother dear –
> Look, he knows us, ain't he queer?'
> 'Hush, my own, don't talk so wild;
> That's your father, dearest child.'
> 'That's my father? No such thing,'
> Father died away last spring.'
> 'Father didn't die, you dub;
> Father joined a golfing club.
> Now the club is closed, so he
> Has no place to go, you see.
> No place left for him to roam,
> That is why he's coming home.'

One of the homewreckers in golf clubs has to be the men's bar. This is the great watering hole for the golfing heroes, secluded from the glare of the ladies, talking men's chat, and in many cases forgetting the last words of their wives as they left their homes, 'Now don't be late for lunch, mother is coming today. The last time you came home late the joint was ruined and the whole family upset, so don't let it happen again.'

Of course, Harry manages to win a few bob, and is in a highly elated state and after a few gin and tonics he suddenly remembers 'lunch,' and probably downs a couple more before he leaves to meet the onslaught from his wife, the stoney glare from his mother-in-law (both rightly so), and generally an atmosphere over lunch, after which he falls into a deep sleep and wakes up like an anti-Christ.

However, coming back to the title of this chapter, I don't know who said it in the first place, but whoever it was certainly had good reasoning because in my world where I have been fortunate, or unfortunate, to meet a lot of famous people, I have found most of them a complete pain in the neck, and certainly would not want to invite any of them back to my home unless it was to show off to the neighbours or impress people by the fact that I knew them.

Fortunately, they are not all like that, and a number of them are very interesting people and pleasant when it suits them. There are some that I always remember, and who stick out in my mind. Douglas Bader was one, and I recall playing golf with him when he was a low handicap golfer, in fact I think it was four, and how he managed to hit the ball so well and get around with two artificial legs was really remarkable. He would never take any assistance to the extent of being rude, and I recall two instances which happened during one of the BBC pro-celebrity golf tournaments, which that year was held at Turnberry.

The sponsor of that particular event was Mr Jack Aisher of Marley Tile fame and he had kindly loaned his helicopter to the wives of the participants for aerial flights around the area, which was very beautiful. My wife and Douglas's wife decided to join a party and make this trip, word of which came to Douglas's ears when we were all having lunch together. He said to his wife, 'You are not going up in the helicopter until I have checked out the pilot.' This he did by duly subjecting the unfortunate man to an intensive grilling, after which he returned and said, 'I am not impressed, you are not going up,' and indeed she did not go, albeit it she was embarrassed and upset about it.

Douglas then carried on and was a participant playing with the professional in one of the events which was for television, when unfortunately he suffered a very nasty heart attack whilst in a bunker, the other celebrity was Bruce Forsyth. He was taken and put to bed at the hotel and told to stay there, and when I went to see him he looked awful, and uttered the words, 'Don't worry – I'll be all right.'

That evening I was standing in the foyer of the hotel waiting for some people to have a pre-dinner drink, when who should come down the stairs regaled in his black tie and dinner jacket but Douglas Bader! What could one say it would be a brave man who would utter the words 'You don't look too well should you be down here this evening?' Anyway, he joined us for dinner, stayed as long as anyone and was fine the next day, and indeed lived after that event for many years.

Another very intense and dedicated golfer I met and played with was Gary Player. To understand his intensity and dedication one had to actually be playing with him, and you could feel it in the atmosphere like sparks. His concentration never let up, and that is why he has been at the top for so long, and even today in the seniors tournaments and elsewhere he is showing that he is still one of the best players in the world. What a great example he shows to the other sixty-three old professionals and to other people as well. I remember in March 1973 the two of us opened the La Manga complex in Spain, and he was rather upset by two things. One that I was driving about thirty yards further than him, and also that I shot a sixty-six against his sixty-eight. Afterwards he called a press conference, which was typical Gary and very funny. I remained good friends with him and I had contact with him again during the difficult years with South Africa, particularly from a sporting side, and he was a great ambassador who managed to keep all the various parties intact. To his eternal credit he never emigrated, and kept on playing for South Africa despite all the brickbats. I wish him well and I know he will go on playing for many years and win many more tournaments.

'The Ice Man' is my name for another great golfing character I was fortunate to meet in Augusta at one of the Masters – Ben Hogan. Clinically I have no doubt he was the greatest golfer the world has ever seen and how he could train himself to produce the accuracy with such regularity will always be a source of wonderment to any who are fortunate enough to have watched him. I can remember sitting having tea with him on the lawns outside that famous club house at Augusta – and by the way, he was always Mister Hogan, never Ben and at the end of our conversation, he said, 'Well, is there anything I can do for you Tommie?' to which I replied, 'I would like you to give me a tip from that great repertoire of yours.'

His advice in answer to this was, 'Remember, you always hit the ball with the top part of your left arm.' That is a very technical and boring statement for people who do not play golf, but he summed up all the basic rudiments of the golf swing in that one remark. It was a fascinating meeting and I shall always remember it with great pride.

Ireland has always been full of great characters and one of my favourites and a great friend who was still going strong in the mid seventies was Joe Carr; arguably one of the greatest amateur golfers of all time, and his achievements are well chronicled. However, I would like to relate one instance which occurred after he had won his first British Open Amateur Championship at St Andrews. This was a great thing for the country, a wonderful achievement, and his golf club felt they would like to do something to remember him by. It was decided to have a portrait painted for him. A whip-round took place and a sum of money was raised to have the work done. The next task was deciding whom they should commission, and the choice was Sean O'Sullivan, at that time a world famous artist whose portraits were worked in crayon, and whose works hung in art galleries throughout the world. Everyone wondered what would be the best approach, because Sean was 'very fond of a drop', to use an Irish expression, and could be seen each day in a well known Dublin hostelry. You had to get to him before twelve noon because after that he would certainly not have been interested, being well into his daily consumption of alcohol.

It was decided that the captain of the club would make the approach, which he duly did, arriving at the pub at ten to twelve, whereupon he found the great Sean sitting on a stool and crouched over the bar in a typical posture, his head resting on his elbow. Michael, the captain, was a little nervous of approaching the great man, so he finally went up to him and introduced himself, then gave his little spiel about the great accomplishments of Joe winning this great championship, and the fame he had brought to his country. He then went on to ask him to do a portrait, explaining about the money raised from the members of the golf club. At the end of this speech there was a grunt from O'Sullivan which amounted to two words, 'How much?' to which Michael explained that the club had raised sixty pounds – a great deal of money in those days. This was followed by a perceptible pause – O'Sullivan never having even turned to face the captain – and out came another grunt, 'I wouldn't whitewash his arse for that!' So that was the end of that! Michael went off with his tail between his legs and eventually the picture was painted by someone else. Indeed, it is there in the clubhouse to be seen to this day.

Brendan Behan was another character who was too fond of a drop, and I used to meet him occasionally in Dublin. Because he was who he was he got away with murder at times for things which would have landed anyone else in serious trouble or even prison. That's the sort of person he was. I recall one instance in Grafton Street, Dublin, when I was walking with him up the street on the right hand side and coming down on the other side was a well-know titled lady, very elegantly dressed and wearing a lovely red hat and trailing two little corgis on a lead. Everyone was turning to look at her, knowing who she was, and she knew that. Suddenly the air was shattered by a roar from Behan, 'How are ya, Betsy? You look great today – you know the old saying, 'red hat, no drawers', which literally brought Grafton Street to a stop. She fixed Behan with a look, and if looks could kill he would have been dead, but it sent the whole street into gales of laughter. I mentioned it to her some time later, and it seems she had relented and thought it was very funny. He would go into a bar where there would be some ladies he didn't know, and he would make all sorts of terrible statements, and squeeze certain parts of their anatomy. On another occasion I remember in this lovely house he had broken an antique chair, and was then sick into the fire. Awful things to have done, but things like this were accepted by people because of who he was, and they still invited him to parties even though he would create havoc, just to be able to say they had had Brendan Behan there. Alcohol killed him in the end, but his name will go on for ever.

In the states I met Jack Dempsey in his famous bar, and Joe DiMaggio, who was married to Marilyn Monroe. Closer to home, a wonderful character who never changes is Henry Cooper, our own ex-heavyweight champion; always pleasant, ever smiling, and who does a great deal for charity.

Away from the sporting world I have already spoken of Mrs Gandhi, one of the most beautiful women I have ever met. I came back from America one time by sea with Danny Kaye, a great world entertainer. He was sitting at my table but had very little to say and hardly ever smiled. He said that he had never told a funny story in any of his shows, which if you think about it is absolutely correct. He had a wonderful way of putting things across and was a real genius, but you cannot ever recall him saying, 'Have you heard this one…' On that occasion he was travelling to London for his second big showing at the London Palladium, having had a wonderful reception the previous time. He invited me along, and sent me tickets for the front row for what a absolute smash hit, and the papers next day ran the headline, 'The biggest hit since Danny Kaye'.

You find with comedians in general that off stage they are a different animal altogether. There's no doubt about it that some of them are much more funny in normal circumstances. Two which come to my mind are Bruce Forsyth and Jimmy Tarbuck – an evening with them is an absolute riot and their spontaneity is quite remarkable. Both are very enthusiastic and useful golfers, I might add.

I have met many cricketers including the great West Indian, Sir Leary Constantine, who I was fortunate enough to play against in a representative match in Ireland, at which I had the honour of getting him out LBW. Unfortunately, he wouldn't go out, and after a consultation with the umpire, during which he said he wasn't ready or something to that effect, he did stay on. Afterwards, when he was down at my end he said, 'Just remember all these people here came to see me, son, not you!' When I was playing in Ireland there was one wonderful old character called Mucker Burn who frequently appeared in the role of umpire. He was rather deaf and I remember on one occasion asking him how many balls there were to go in the over because I had lost count, and he replied, 'Half past three sir.' Off the field we used to give him the odd pint and a few shillings, which could work wonders if it came to a close decision, but he was a honourable and great old character and we all loved him very much.

My sporting hero of the moment is our young grandson, Scott, whose enthusiasm and dedication have provided me with many hours of joy and pleasure. This is what sport and entertainment should be all about and it would be a sad and sorry world without it.

Chapter Twelve
A Price to Pay

'Do you want to creep and crawl through the second half of your life?' This was one of the most significant things ever said to me, spoken by our family doctor, who was also a close personal friend. I had been going through a very rough period in my life, and indeed was still going through it, which was the accumulation of twenty years of hurtling round the world, taking on board all the problems that one endeavours to resolve with business, fighting law cases, dealing with bad people, and life in general.

Looking back I did not take heed of the 'traffic light' which I maintain is within everybody. There are times when it shines red and times when it shines green. If you ignore the red light, which is something I'm afraid I did, then you do so at your peril. Quite simply, I had never really learned how to relax properly.

It all happened one evening when I was driving home from my business on a perfectly normal summer's day. Suddenly I felt this prickly heat coming over me and fortunately had enough leave of my senses to pull across and stop the car. It was a sensation that I had not had before, but I was to have it many times afterwards, and I was certain it was a massive heart attack on the way. All sorts of things flashed through my mind at that moment, and I was convinced I was going to die.

My system apparently decided I was not going to die

after all, but that it would turn off the switch for a while, and I just blacked out. I came to a short while afterwards with a massive headache. I decided then that I was capable of getting home, but that I would not tell anyone what had happened but try and get through it on my own. What I didn't know, or realise at the time, was that I was pretty far down the line to a nervous breakdown.

The attacks became a regular occurrence, and one of the worst features was the fear of the recurrences, because my mind associated them with certain times and places. They were followed by claustrophobia, also a fear of going out of the house, and worst of all for me – because of my business – a fear of flying.

The blackouts became more frequent and one of them occurred in a church, which meant I didn't go back into one of those for a very long time. I went to the cinema in Dublin to see *Reach for the Sky*, the story of Douglas Bader. About halfway through the film I felt the sensation coming over me, and had to get out. I managed to make it to the foyer before I passed out, and in the process I hit my head on the floor, which must have extended my period of blackout. I remember coming round and through the haze looking up at the figure of a priest, who had been called to the scene by the people who saw it happen. He was convinced I was dying and was in the process of administering the Last Rites to me. It was a very embarrassing and awful experience, with all the people gazing at me wondering whether they should call an ambulance, and whether I would live.

On top of the blackouts my sleeping pattern was all shot to pieces. I was eating badly, and in fact my whole nervous system seemed totally uncoordinated and in a horrible mess. It was decided the time had come to seek proper medical assistance, which I did, and in fact I saw a number of specialists. Once aware of my lifestyle they came to the conclusion the best solution was to slow me down by throwing a few pills at the problem. The pills did me no good, in fact I think they made me worse, and when I mentioned this fact to the medical people they decided I needed something stronger, and so it went on.

Looking back, I don't really know what else I could have done, but I carried on with my work under the shadow of this affliction, dreading meetings, having to go out, looking for excuses not to fly, and wondering where it was all going to end. On top of everything else I had started suffering from migraines, which I had never had in my life before, and the first one hit me whilst I was driving the car with my family to watch a football match in which our eldest son was playing. That started another cycle of events and they became so bad that I could only go into a dark room and wait for it all to pass over. Those who have gone through this trauma will know the after-effects can last for some time and are not at all pleasant.

One of the worst migraines happened in the middle of an important golf game in County Dublin and I had to give the match to my opponent and ask for assistance to the clubhouse, which was highly embarrassing in front of all those people. Worst of all it set up the cycle of thought which centred round, *Is this going to happen to me every time I go on a golf course?*

This went on for over ten years, and had become a way of life. One day something nudged me to ring up our family GP, whose name was Dennis Keane, and I asked if I could call to see him. We had a long discussion and, being a very practical chap, he said in his opinion I was not becoming physically tired but my heart was still in good condition, and what I had gone through would probably have killed off three or four normal people! He advised me to throw away all the pills and get out and play cricket or whatever to try and bring my system back into some short of shape. Easy words I suppose at the time, but at the end of it he uttered those significant words which opened up this chapter. 'Tommie, you are forty years of age, the best years of your life are in front of you. Do you want to creep and crawl through the second half of your life?'

I decided to give it a go, knowing there would be times when I would take one step forward and two steps back. Indeed there were occasions when I took one step forward and three steps back, but I was absolutely determined to do as he had said. The important thing which he had got through to me and to my system was that I was not going to die. This certainly took away some of the fear and I remember going out of the house for the first time without the horrible little green pills rattling round in my pocket, and wondering if I would make it. Then came an occasion which I feel was one of the turning points in my life. It emulated from a large business arrangement which was in the final stages of negotiation and required me to travel to Bombay in India, and I knew there was no backing down.

This resurrected all the fears of flying and the length of time it would take, the inner turmoil was awful. However, I knew I had to go and my good wife Kate came along with me. I shall never forget waiting for take off in a BOAC VC10 at Heathrow, and as we raced down the runway and tore off into the sky I went through the tortures of the damned.

The trip was very successful, not only business-wise but also privately, arising from an introduction to their family guru, whom I mentioned earlier in the book as being the most famous in India and the world at that time. He had just been working with the Beatles a few weeks before, and I went along to see him and explained my problems, which he took on board with no emotion whatsoever. He just said, 'You have allowed yourself to become one of the victims of the modern era, and unless you learn how to relax naturally without the aid of pills, you will end up a wreck.'

Over the next few days he taught me many things about relaxation: what to do at the end of the day, and how to do it, and what to do if I ever felt this feeling coming over me again. Looking back now I realise what a great man and healer he was. If what he said to me could be packaged it would be a best seller. From there on, slowly but surely I got better and better, but it took a long time to be able to go back into church again and sit for a while, to go to the cinema or theatre, but I knew I had to conquer it. One of the things the guru said to me I will always remember, though I sometimes momentarily forget, and that was, 'Make sure you reverse your life into the future, looking back at the mistakes you have made in the past and make sure you don't make them again.'

Going back over this period I have reflected on a number of things, and one of them centres around the word 'sympathy'. When you are generally in a low state you tend to look for this, difficult though it may be to find, but don't do it. 'Pull yourself together' is a well-known statement and one said to me on many occasions. I also learned that people are not really interested, and why should they be? They just don't want to know because they have their own lives to live and will say whatever they feel you want to hear. The message from all this is you have to do it all yourself, and if you can really find one friend in all this who is really concerned and tries to help you, then you are a lucky person. If you can go to your grave or whatever with one or two good friends then you have had a successful life. You will make a lot of acquaintances and meet a lot of people but very, very few real friends. I certainly found that out.

I managed to stay that particular course through the bad times, and I can see similar situations frequently in other people, even in my own family, but you cannot say anything to them because they don't want to know. You see it practically everywhere you go, driving on the roads with the tension on people's faces, the white knuckles and the air of 'must get there at all costs', and you think how much better they would be if they could speak to someone like the guru. When I see all the cars racing away in the mornings I wonder how many of the trips are really necessary, if they left themselves enough time they wouldn't have to tear along at high speeds. I see the same thing in supermarkets where people are on a high and if you bump into them they turn on you as if you had attacked them. The whole culture is one of hostility born out of the pace of modern life today, unhappy associations, unhappy marriages, and yet one sees no real effort by the authorities to alleviate the problems such as traffic, noise etc. and make it easier to go places, or to deal with those people who are affecting other people's lives.

When you take a city like London, where I lived for eleven years, you see the absolute consternation, frustration and congestion every single hour of every single day. Yet when some old head of state comes to town and decides he wants to be seen going from A to B, all the streets are cleared and the entourage drives along as if nothing was happening, never thinking of the disruption behind the scenes with all the road blocks and whatever which results from these occasions.

Looking back on this chapter of my life I think one of the most important lessons I had to learn (and I'm not saying that I'm perfect in any way) is, 'Be tolerant and try not to allow certain things to get inside you, or they will burn you away and haunt you, wake you in the middle of the night.' This is self discipline which you must work out for yourself, and as you get on in years try not to be cynical, this is something I have to fight all the time, since the mixture inside me is a bit of a complex one and it also has a liberal helping of some explosive substance that tends to go off every now and then. But I am getting better – I am at peace with myself a lot more than before, and I hope I am a better person for all that.

At this point I will end the 'gospel according to Tommie' and try to practise what I preach!

Chapter Thirteen
Keep On Keeping On

Most people assume you should be retired at a certain age; it's an accepted thing. I am asked the question all the time which makes me wonder if I look that old! My answer is 'no' without any elaboration because I believe you must keep the old brainbox ticking over all the time. No staying in bed until mid morning, not bothering to shave and generally looking like an imitation peasant. When you reach that stage you are waiting to die. Not for me, thank you.

Age comes into everyone's life, when one realises and reflects that each of us grows older by the minute. Age embraces many things, including being probably the one secret a woman can always keep, but to me it remains significant of a number of levels. One should never complain about old age because an awful lot of people never had the privilege to reach it.

As I mentioned earlier in the chapter about the Indian guru, you can look back on your life and what sustains you, so I would like in the finale of this book to bring to light what has kept me going and what continues to do so.

I have never allowed myself to be superstitious, which can be contagious to a number of people, and indeed one very good friend of mine, a good cricketer, never went anywhere without a rabbit's foot in his pocket. I don't know where he got it or whether in fact it was a real one, but he used to say to me, 'Tommie, you should get one of these,' and I would pull his leg and remark, 'It didn't work very well for the rabbit, did it!' I have always had a simple belief that the best thing to keep for good luck is some money at the bank.

Coming back to answer this question which is always put to me, my reply is, 'No, I'm not retired but I do not do as much as I used to for obvious reasons.' I like to keep on keeping on, and have no desire to wake up in the morning wondering what I am going to do with myself for the rest of the day or the rest of the week. I like to have something to look forward to, being a competitive person I like to achieve new things, and I suppose that writing this book is a good example of that.

To be honest, I believe the real answer lies in one word – emotion. It is a mental state with many parts such as fear, excitement, love, recreation, precision, to name some of the important ones. I think the strongest in my case was fear. It came into my early days as a Protestant in a hostile community, where it walked beside me every day, it came in later years watching friends die of cancer and wondering whether I was going to be next. In sport if you have never felt the shiver of fear or nervousness on a big occasion, then you have never really participated.

By sheer doggedness I managed to convince my inner man that I was not going to let fear rule my life, and that I must be the governor, and I exercise that option to the supreme limit no matter what is happening. I also learned that it is vital to focus on what you are doing, particularly as you get older, and in tandem with this to concentrate on what you are doing otherwise you forget all sorts of things. Your mind wanders and you can have silly accidents.

I would also like to mention again the word 'sympathy', because I found out that if you look for it and receive it when you are ill (and I don't mean here ill with some malignant condition which can recur) you will never get better. If you are getting over a condition then allow yourself to slip back into talking about it and seeking sympathy, it triggers off the problem once again and you go backwards. I have done this many, many times, and it is a most difficult exercise just to say, 'Yes, I'm feeling very well thank you very much.'

It is essential to get to know the nervous and muscular systems in your body and how they behave and even function. Everyone has the 'inner doctor' whom they have to trust, and you have to learn how to overcome anxiety about your health. In this context one of my greatest fears relates to any operational remedy to any part of my body, and this arises from some rather painful experiences I have had in the past.

Three instances come to my mind. The first was in my early twenties when I was diagnosed by a medical man – I will call him that at this time – wrongly, as it subsequently turned out, as having a grumbling appendix. At that time I was spending a large percentage of the year away in rural areas where medical amenities were very scarce and it was deemed a wise thing to have it removed, which I did. They were not so good in those days as they are now, so a period of post-operation rest was prescribed. Being a private patient, I was supposed to have a private room but a clerical error, which undoubtedly saved my life, resulted in me having to share a room.

I was brought there after the operation and during the 'coming round' period a young nurse was assigned to hold my tongue in order to prevent it falling back down my throat. Things were going to plan until another young nurse called my lassie outside for some reason or other, which meant that she let go my tongue, and of course it slipped down my throat. Fortunately my co-resident noticed my face turning black, and funny noises coming from my throat. He jumped out of his bed, realising there was no time to lose, and proceeded to retrieve my tongue, even though he himself was very ill. Without his action I wouldn't be around today, and yet there was no apology from the hospital or anything like that.

The second incident was about six or seven years later when I discovered a very sore type of blister on my posterior, which the doctor originally had said was a bee sting. I was not too bothered about this thing, but it turned out to be something more serious and I was told I had to go to hospital to undergo the maximum injection of penicillin that a human being could have! It was like being hit by a double-decker bus – I shall never forget it – my whole system went bananas, just as if I had had a massive electric shock, and I remember thinking, *This is one hell of a bee sting!* However, a few more days passed, and I was told to go to hospital again where they gave me some sort of medication. I remember going into the operating theatre on one of the trolleys and wondering in my half doped condition what the hell was going on.

What was going on was that they had called in this surgeon who had a look at the 'bee string' and diagnosed that I had cancer of the bowel and had to be operated on immediately! It turned out his identification of the disease was totally wrong, but the pain that endured afterwards for weeks and indeed for the rest of my life, was a legacy that I shall never forget. My screams of agony could be heard all over the hospital – it was quite indescribable. Yet again I recovered no apology whatsoever. Later on it was discovered I had contracted a bacterial problem from a dirty toilet seat, and I often wondered afterwards how many people go through these problems because of the disgraceful state of toilets used by members of the public in this country.

A short while ago the heel of my right foot was giving me a lot of grief and interrupting my golf which I continued to play in agony, but thank goodness I did. It got so bad I went along to the experts who told me I had 'policeman's heel', something I had never heard of, which turned out to be some sort of growth. They said I needed in operation to remove it and that I would have to walk on sticks or crutches for about six months. Fortunately, I was continuing to play golf, I had commitments which had to be kept. I went for a game with an old friend of mine, a medical man in the RAF, and we were playing on his home course. I was relating this incident to him, when he said, 'Don't have anything to do with the operation. What you do is get one of these medical heels which you put into your shoe, cut a hole in it to take the pressure of the area which is hurting and see what happens.' I can tell you that it very quickly started to get better and within three weeks was completely gone. If I had not gone to play golf that day I would have been hobbling around for months! Needless to say after these experiences, I always try to avoid the knife.

What keeps me going? I think most people of my age get all different types of pains. Having played a lot of sport and still continuing to play a fair amount I get pains in my shoulders, parts of my back, my knees and legs, and the easy way out would be to do what I see others doing – to take painkillers – but I have never done that. As long as I know that these aches are not terminal and can't kill me immediately, I will take them on. I believe that if I do this and trust that 'doctor' that's inside each one of us, the pains will get bored and go away. I can imagine people now saying, 'What a load of nonsense – he wouldn't be saying that if he had my pains,' but I'm just saying that I have always tackled it by saying, 'Bugger you, you're not going to get me down.' Don't look for sympathy, and don't tell anyone you have the pains, and mind over matter without any shadow of a doubt helps. I will close that by saying that you must not let fear rule your life but always remember pain is a warning.

Then we come to other emotions like excitement, which is a great stimulant to your own nervous system. Different things excite different people, the achievement of winning something, whatever it may be, going to the races and seeing your horse winning, your son winning at his local sports – it is all a great stimulant, love – the love of your family and the kindness that goes with it, which I think is even more important in life than love. Sometimes people get love mixed up with physical attraction, which is not a lasting recipe for success. Add to this some recreation, whatever it may be. Everyone has their own 'yoga', whether it be doing the garden, going for walks, playing bridge, listening to music. All part of that wonderful fabric of life.

Finally, one thing that has always been a major part of my makeup is precision. I like things to be precise, and must know where I am going, what I am doing, and to plan things well. But again you have to be tolerant, and understand that other people in this world can be different and you can't expect the same things from them as you expect from yourself.

If you can put all these things together – and make sure you keep your bowels loose – you are in with a good chance! You don't have to give thanks every day for good health because you are entitled to it. This body we have is a very resilient thing and can take a lot of hardship and punishment. As long as you give it a reasonable amount of care, attention, rest and food it will perform better than any other machine the world has ever invented.

Looking back over my life to date I suppose one could rightly say, 'That guy has had as many lives as a cat,' reading all the things that have happened and could have happened. But I'm still here and would like to add to all the other things I've said that eternal vigilance is very necessary, particularly when you leave home and when you travel, and meet strange people. I thought I was pretty good at that, having travelled the world, until one evening in a five-star London hotel I was having an nightcap at the bar after attending some meetings. The barman introduced me to a lady and her daughter who were sitting there. We chatted for a while, then I said cheerio and went off to bed. I woke up the next morning about half past ten with one of the porters shaking me and discovered that the lady in question, in cahoots with the barman, had drugged my drink and stolen a very valuable watch and money that I had. Afterwards the doctor told me that she had given me a dose which could very easily have killed me and I could not stop going to sleep for about five days afterwards. It took me a long time to get over it, and it just shows you never to be too careful and don't trust anybody you don't know.

As I wind up this chapter I am in good shape for my three score years and ten, I still lead a very active life, taking one day at a time. I don't see myself with any clock on the mantelpiece bearing a retirement inscription. I shall endeavour to do my best as long as I am above the ground because once that effort stops everything else goes. The graveyards are full of men of whom it was said, 'the world couldn't get along without them,' I'm sure they will never say that about me!